A new book in
THE JOSSEY-BASS SERIES
IN HIGHER EDUCATION

QUALITY EDUCATION FOR LESS MONEY

How can colleges improve their financial position and retain or increase the quality of education they offer? This new source-book shows college administrators how to employ a proven planning strategy based upon a highly successful technique of college management—cost effectiveness.

Cost effectiveness, as Richard Meeth shows, does not imply efficiency experts or institutional researchers as college presidents. Cost effectiveness involves gathering the necessary data to determine where money is being spent, developing corresponding plans to see to it that only expenses essential to quality and purpose remain, and making necessary institutional changes without destroying morale.

In his new book, Meeth presents the full report of his study of sixty-six colleges that agreed to use the author's cost-effectiveness strategy. Drawing on real-life examples, Meeth shows other colleges how they too can use cost analysis to bring expenditures in line with income. He provides all the necessary data collection forms and comparative tables that make implementation an uncomplicated procedure. He also makes twelve specific recommendations which, although controversial in extent, prove that all colleges can reduce costs, improve effici-

Quality Education for Less Money

ᗷᗷᗷᗷᗷᗷ

A Sourcebook for Improving Cost Effectiveness

ency, and retain the effectiveness of the programs they offer. The sixty-six colleges realized great gains from the use of Meeth's strategy of cost effectiveness among them, the collective saving of over one million dollars.

Other colleges can do the same. College administrators who read this book, follow these procedures, and draw up their own cost studies will have something to show when they go seeking further funds. There is no survival insurance for private higher education today, but if colleges follow Meeth's strategies and recommendations, as the colleges reported here have done, they will have the most reliable policy currently available.

THE AUTHOR

L. RICHARD MEETH is associate professor of higher education at the State University of New York at Buffalo.

L. Richard Meeth

Foreword by

Roger J. Voskuyl

QUALITY EDUCATION FOR LESS MONEY

 Jossey-Bass Publishers

San Francisco · Washington · London · 1974

QUALITY EDUCATION FOR LESS MONEY
A Sourcebook for Improving Cost Effectiveness
by L. Richard Meeth

Copyright © 1974 by: Jossey-Bass, Inc., Publishers
615 Montgomery Street
San Francisco, California 94111
&
Jossey-Bass Limited
3 Henrietta Street
London WC2E 8LU

Library of Congress Catalogue Card Number LC 73-18502

International Standard Book Number ISBN 0-87589-211-6

Manufactured in the United States of America

JACKET DESIGN BY WILLI BAUM

FIRST EDITION

Code 7406

The Jossey-Bass
Series in Higher Education

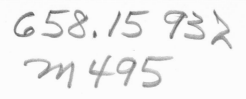

Consulting Editor

HAROLD L. HODGKINSON, *University of California, Berkeley*

To my wife, Sally

ㅈㅈㅈㅋㅋㅋ

Foreword

Sidney G. Tickton, in his report *Needed: A Ten-Year College Budget* (published by the Fund for the Advancement of Education in 1961), urged colleges to "focus attention on the budget outlook up to ten years ahead." Heeding his words, the Council for the Advancement of Small Colleges (CASC) readily encouraged its members to make such long-range projections of their budget requirements, and in 1969 it sponsored a planning project under the direction of Tickton and Earl J. McGrath. In the course of this project, a strong conviction arose on the part of CASC that the projections were not giving adequate treatment to the crucial element of cost analysis in the instructional area—an area that can account for 40 to 50 percent of the total budget of a college. Fortunately, Thad L. Hungate and L. Richard Meeth (1964) had developed the concept of cost analysis in instructional areas, and this concept was subsequently built into the CASC project. To date, over one hundred colleges have participated in this cost project. Data on sixty-six of these colleges are reported in this book.

Cost analysis, such as Meeth discusses here, has become one of the most valuable tools of the administrator for making decisions of both short- and long-term significance. Static enrollments, mounting costs, and deficit budgets require current data that can be used as a basis for major decisions. None are so delicate or critical as those within the area of instructional programs.

The colleges that have put to effective use the cost analysis program developed by Meeth have discovered some startling facts: colleges in the same geographical area with equivalent enrollments, tuition, and budgets can show differentials of up to $2000 in average salary; a deficit can be traced to the fact that a college is offering twice as many majors as other schools of its size; costs can be reduced when colleges cooperate on a curricular program in a specific field instead of each college's running its own; one unit of difference in the student-faculty ratio can make a great difference in salary expenditures. These are just a few of the problem areas that cost analysis has uncovered. Chapter Six, on the uses of cost analysis, brings other possibilities for reducing costs into sharp focus.

We are pleased to make available in this book a tool which every college president and dean can use to achieve more efficient operation of his institution. We are grateful to the Alfred P. Sloan Foundation and to the LeTourneau Foundation for supporting the publication and distribution of this report.

ROGER J. VOSKUYL
Executive Director
Council for the Advancement of Small Colleges

꙰꙰꙰꙰꙰꙰

Preface

On a recent trip from Washington, D.C., our plane taxied onto the takeoff runway as usual, then suddenly turned around and returned to the loading ramp. The door opened; pilot, maintenance staff, and stewardess conferred briefly; the door shut; and within minutes we were in the air on our way to Buffalo. I asked the stewardess what had happened. She answered, "The pilot said something was wrong with one of the engines." I said, amazed, "It certainly didn't take long to fix!" She replied, "Oh, it wasn't fixed; we just changed pilots!"

This story is a parable of the liberal arts college today. Over and over again, instead of working on the fundamental economic and educational problems that have beset them, colleges simply change personnel—as though new leadership can somehow fly on with only half power. This book describes what happened to a group of institutions, representative of all liberal arts colleges, which had the courage to lay themselves open to scrutiny and reform their future.

In 1972, when most colleges were suffering to some extent from reductions in income and from rising costs, these institutions—sixty-six private, nonselective, relatively small liberal arts colleges offering the B.A. degree—agreed to participate in a cost-effectiveness study sponsored by the Council for the Advancement of Small Colleges. The results of that study, which are largely applicable to all liberal arts colleges and universities, are reported here.

Chapter One, a preliminary discussion, considers the strange resistance to planning in our society.

Chapters Two through Five document the results of the analyses of the participating colleges and provide comparative tables for colleges beginning the cost study. More specifically, Chapter Two describes the participating institutions and the methodology of the study and then focuses on curriculum and its related costs in these institutions. Chapter Three discusses sources of income and distribution of expenditures in fifty-six of the participating colleges; and Chapter Four discusses the relationship of expenditure and income in the admissions and development offices of fifty-eight of these colleges. Chapter Five examines the concepts of efficiency and effectiveness and applies them to three pairs of colleges in the study, in order to determine whether high-cost colleges are in fact more effective than low-cost colleges.

As is noted in Chapter Six, "The sixty-six colleges in this cost-effectiveness study demonstrated great gains from their participation." This chapter summarizes those gains—among them, the collective saving of over one million dollars a year.

Chapter Seven details terminology and procedures and proposes a strategy whereby other colleges can develop their own program of cost effectiveness, incorporated in a comprehensive long-range plan. Numerous sample tables and data-collection forms are provided here, so that institutions can undertake their own analyses.

Finally, Chapter Eight pulls together the conclusions of the cost studies and makes specific recommendations designed to reduce costs and to increase efficiency without impairing the effectiveness of the programs being offered in liberal arts colleges today.

I am deeply indebted to the Council for the Advancement of Small Colleges for asking me to undertake this study, to the participating institutions for their eagerness to know the truth about themselves, to Richard LeTourneau and his family foundation for underwriting the cost of preparing this report, and to the Sloan Foundation for help in subsidizing publication and distribution costs.

Roger Voskuyl, executive director of CASC, gave invaluable support to the entire project. Without his efforts and encouragement this record could not have been compiled. In like manner Harold Hodgkinson—editor, critic, reader, statistician, and friend—suggested many important additions and revisions which strengthened this report. I owe much to both these men for their help in this and other projects with liberal arts colleges.

No professor ought to engage in research which is not, partially at least, relevant to his teaching and advising. This study could not possibly have been completed were it not a group project—graduate students and professor, but mostly graduate students. Robert Knott was responsible for most of the research and much of the writing for Chapter Five. David Spence prepared all the summary tables, the statistical analysis, and the admissions survey. Robert Hausrath and Roy Pipitone handled many of the initial individual analyses, and Robert Webber took charge of the bibliographic research and the follow-up analysis of uses of the data. I think these students benefited from their collaborations. I know that I did, and I am grateful for their work, especially for the ensuing friendships and insights into how colleges work. This collective effort has confirmed once again the value of a team working to solve the problems of higher education.

Others also participated in the completion of this manuscript. William Jellema, then of the Association of American Colleges; Stanley Idzerda, president of the College of St. Benedict; Gordon Werkema, associate executive director of CASC; and Walter Hobbs, assistant professor of higher education, SUNY/Buffalo, served as an advisory review panel and offered many helpful editorial suggestions.

Finally, Jackie Rance typed three drafts of the report and all the tables for each participating college. I appreciate their efforts, especially the obvious concern that all shared for the future well-being of liberal arts colleges.

Vesuvius, Virginia   L. RICHARD MEETH
January 1974

❧❧❧❦❦❦

Contents

Foreword
Roger J. Voskuyl   ix

Preface   xi

1. The Problem with Planning   1

2. Cost Analysis of Curricula   6

xv

3. Income and Expenditure 47

4. Admissions and Development Costs 59

5. Efficiency and Effectiveness
   with Robert E. Knott 74

6. Uses of Cost Analysis 99

7. A Comprehensive Planning Strategy 120

8. Recommendations for Effectiveness 154

General Bibliography 175

Annotated Bibliography 193

Index 203

Quality Education for Less Money

⅍⅍⅍⅍⅍⅍

A Sourcebook for Improving

Cost Effectiveness

Chapter I

ᚾᚾᚾᚲᚲᚲ

The Problem
with Planning

N o one who writes about the future of the liberal arts college re-
futes the need for institutional research, cost analysis, and short- and
long-range planning. Every author in the bibliography of this book,
as well as every president and chief academic officer in every private
college visited in this project, espouses the need for planning based
on careful institutional analysis. Yet such planning, however much
praised, is not widely practiced in private higher education.

1

Institutional research and short- and long-range planning have been, to a greater or lesser extent, available to practitioners and professors of higher education for at least a century. Efforts at cost analysis, the heart of this book, are more recent, dating back to the beginning of this century. Witmer (1972) has amply documented the history of cost studies in American higher education. He reports that unit instructional costs were computed as early as 1894 for city school expenditures and that, in 1915, a report on expenditures at the University of Wisconsin resulted in conclusions expressed in terms of costs per full-time student. Since 1915, cost studies have been pouring forth from educational researchers and economists at the rate of about one a month somewhere in the United States. A large body of sometimes contradictory, sometimes confirming literature has been developed to aid colleges and universities in institutional research and cost analysis. But in spite of the many studies and models available to administrators of private colleges, very little institutional research or planning takes place. Of the sixty-six colleges for which cost studies were prepared in the course of the project described in this book (approximately an 8 percent sample of all private liberal arts colleges in the United States), very few had plans in 1970 to steer them through any part of this decade; few knew such basic information about themselves as average class size, faculty-student ratio by department, or cost per student credit hour.

Although a number of institutions in the nation *have* attempted to plan, their aborted efforts lie at the bottom of a file drawer or on the shelf in the library. Other institutions have successfully planned but perceived planning as an activity to be done once and checked off annually. Only a very small portion, perhaps 20 percent of America's private colleges, have effectively developed a plan, based on sound data about themselves and their setting, which is revised at least annually and upon which the institution's leadership acts daily.

Why is such a critical concept as planning, with its related aspects of institutional research and cost analysis, so little practiced by the leadership of colleges whose survival demands it? What is there about planning that is so intolerable even when institutional life requires it? Answers to these questions are complex and perhaps confounding. One theory may help.

The thesis was suggested by a phrase uttered by Howard K. Smith in an ABC news broadcast about the energy crisis. For at least twenty years, he observed, America has been aware of an impending energy crisis but did nothing to mitigate or forestall such a crisis: we did not plan; we only cried. In Smith's words, the nation has "an abhorrence of foresight." This phenomenon seems true of private higher education, if not all postsecondary education. Palola and his associates (Palola, Lehman, and Blischke, 1971) suggest that institutions, administrators, and faculties are very reluctant planners. They come to the task slowly and unprepared; and once gathered at the table, they see planning either as an ineffective means to a desired end or as incompatible with their role and function.

Toffler, in *Future Shock* (1970) and other writings, adequately documents the responses people generate to prospects of the future, noting that the future as an unknown is extremely difficult for people to contemplate. Planning for American higher education most certainly is a task that would engender many of the same responses Toffler cites about the future.

The problem is not alone an educational one. As a nation we have a variety of crises—the energy crisis, the monetary crisis, the silent-majority crisis, the moral crisis, the rise-of-crime crisis, the pollution crisis, and the population crisis—all the results of a lack of planning. All these crises demand attention; but politicians, scientists, social scientists, economists, and other servants of the society find it difficult to plan for our survival. Private higher education is just one of many manifestations of a national phenomenon that is a paradox. In a nation committed to change, to progress, and to expansion, it seems curious that we should be unable or unwilling to utilize the tools and skills most necessary to accomplish these objectives.

This intolerance, this abhorrence of looking ahead, seems to be rooted in our traditions. Traditionally, Americans have been proud of their frontier society. Expansion has been the hallmark of American life since the eastern shores were first invaded. When all the land was pledged, people moved into space, searching for greater freedom of movement and expression. This frontier, expansionist feeling is curtailed by planning. Furthermore, ours is a society that values freedom. Our constitution and our state laws are designed to protect individual freedom and to give each person as much opportunity as possible to move, to think, and to act. But planning curtails personal and collective freedom by forcing participants to choose in advance the alternatives they will pursue, and to commit themselves to those alternatives even though a large number of variables remain unknown. Fear of the unknown is a dominant theme in American literature and psychological and sociological thought. Developing a long-range plan conceivably intensifies that fear because it requires commitment to only one alternative among many, it reduces freedom to choose other alternatives or to withdraw entirely, and it requires colleges with changing leadership to deny fear. Long-range planning generates that fear of commitment to the unknown which it must deny in order to be effective, an intolerable concept in itself.

Beyond the psychological and sociological reasons for the abhorrence of foresight, a number of more mundane reasons can be set forth. Virtually no college administrator, until very recent years at least, has been taught or prepared professionally to undertake the planning task. Faculty and students likewise have grown up in an educational system that places a premium upon modeling and very little value upon problem solving and critical thinking, both central skills in the development of an effective long-range plan. We have not learned the skills or the strategies of planning. In short, people in colleges have not known how to get from here to there.

Good models for planning are few. Most of the models that exist seem too pedestrian, too impractical, too out of touch with reality, or too conservative to allow for creativity, for intuition, or for any freedom of movement. Serious students of planning despair of the plans which colleges, states, and the federal government prepare— either because administrators try to bend reality to fit their pet plan or because they go off and leave a plan in motion without a leader.

If planning is abhorrent to the practitioners of higher education, if our psychological and sociological makeup rejects it and our educational system denies the skills necessary to undertake it, how then can private colleges hope to survive? This book is about a group of colleges that run counter to the society, in which the life urges are stronger than any lost freedom or any fear of the future that may be brought out by planning. With help, this group of institutions undertook careful institutional research and cost analysis as a basis for planning the future. How could this group of colleges—small, nonselective, with few resources and less visibility than most other kinds of institutions in American higher education—undertake as formidable a task as institutional analysis and planning? Perhaps cost analysis and long-range planning are ideas whose time has arrived. Perhaps fear is overcome when survival is clearly at stake. Perhaps the economic and social conditions that precluded the need for planning in higher education during the last decade now force planning upon all institutions.

Chapter II

ㅈㅈㅈㅋㅋㅋ

Cost Analysis
of Curricula

Nearly every private college in America wants to increase the quality and decrease the cost of its educational program. If colleges do not analyze and evaluate their practices, however, the cost will rise without anyone's being able to do anything about it. Fortunately, many colleges are beginning to make studies of their programs and resources; and such studies will enable them to give some direction to the future. For other institutions it is already too late to redeem past failure.

Quantitative facts admittedly do not reveal the quality of education in the colleges studied. These data do not portray the purposes of the institutions. They do not reveal the qualifications of faculty members or measure their dedication to teaching. They do not analyze the quality of the student produced. Descriptive analyses of data related to curriculum, teaching loads, student loads, and costs do, however, provide facts from which an institution can make an analysis of its educational condition and examine the prospects for future development.

Although any college program includes many factors that bear directly upon cost, these differ from one college to another. Objectives, for example, vary in kind and emphasis and, if they are reflected in the educational program, affect cost. Many other institutional features and practices also have an important influence on the cost of an educational effort. The type of academic calendar, the length of the year, the course load a student carries, the scope of the curriculum, the nature of the athletic program, the compensation and teaching load of faculty, the range of and average class size, the techniques of teaching and learning, the library holdings, and a variety of out-of-class and administrative factors bear directly upon the cost.

This chapter focuses on the specifics of the curriculum and its related costs in sixty-six institutions. An initial assessment of the kinds of institutions and methodology is followed by a look at enrollments, credit-hour distribution, majors, courses, faculty, and class size. Costs are reviewed in terms of credit hours and student loads. The chapter concludes with a look at the relationship of cost factors to curricular variables and attempts to assess those relationships that directly affect decision making and planning in small colleges.

The quantitative aspects reviewed here comprise only one year of institutional history. In order to make sound judgments within a single institution, it is important to look at a minimum of three years and perhaps even five. The linear view, instead of comparing with other institutions across the nation for a single year, can give college administrators and faculty a relatively firm picture of the direction in which their institution is moving and provide a reasonably meaningful basis on which to project the next three to five years.

Colleges Studied

The sixty-six institutions that participated in this study are established, reputable, independent, and church-related colleges offering the bachelor's degree. At the time of the study eleven institutions were not accredited by a regional accrediting association. All but four now have correspondent status with their respective associations. The colleges are spread across the nation: fourteen from the Northeast, thirty-three from the Midwest, seven from the West, and twelve from the Southeast. Four of the institutions offer professional programs beyond the bachelor's degree, although no institution offers a master's degree. Thirteen of the institutions are Roman Catholic. Fifty are Protestant and, if not affiliated with a particular denomination, based upon a strong religious commitment. Two institutions maintain no religious ties and are classified as independent. There is one black college in the group. Eleven colleges operate on a quarter system; the remainder follow a semester system, although a large proportion of these institutions have a January term.

Although one participating institution was not a member of the Council for the Advancement of Small Colleges, the colleges were self-selected for the study on the basis of an invitation from the council to all who attended the 1971 national summer workshop. Each college paid a modest fee for a basic analysis (described in Chapter Seven) and agreed to participate in the development of national norms and averages, provided no school in the study would be identified by name.

Based upon the Carnegie Commission reports of Alexander Astin, Calvin B. T. Lee, and C. Robert Pace, institutions participating in this analysis are classified collectively as nonselective, reasonably open-door, liberal arts colleges with a strong religious focus. None of the highly selective, "prestigious," private liberal arts colleges are included. In 1962, however, exactly the same study (See Hungate and Meeth, 1964) conducted with twenty-five selective liberal arts colleges produced virtually the same results in every category, suggesting that selectivity is not a significant factor in most of the variables analyzed here and that private colleges have not changed significantly in the way they structure their offerings and allocate their resources.

Methodology

The methods of investigation employed in this project included collection of data from questionnaires and catalogs, a survey of audits and other financial reports, compilation of statistics based on information provided by questionnaire, follow-up telephone conversations, and verification of data through visits to approximately thirty institutions. Presidents, deans, registrars, business officers, and others in the sixty-six colleges assisted in the collection of the necessary information based on six forms sent to each college (see Chapter Seven).

Each institution was given a set of organized data about itself, which it could use in long-range planning and day-to-day decision making. Colleges of the same general size were grouped on large tables, so that decision makers also could compare themselves with similar institutions in order to get a sense of how they stood nationally. Approximately forty-four different tables were prepared for each college and then interpreted for various members of the administration, faculty, student body, trustees, or alumni. Six regional workshops were held, in which all participating colleges had an opportunity to discuss the nature and meaning of the tables prepared and to correct errors which had developed either from misunderstanding information needed or from mistakes made by project staff in the preparation of the tables.

Questionnaires sent to each institution asked for the name of each course taught in 1970–71; the name and rank of the instructor of each course; whether he was a full-time instructor and, if not, the percent of full-time equivalent; the number of students in each class, laboratory, or section of every course; the number of credits for which the course was offered; the full-time-equivalent enrollment for the year, based on fall figures; tuition charges and other fees; an extensive breakdown of the educational income and expenditures; and the general statement of total income and expenditures. Each college, in addition, was asked to return a catalog marking all courses not offered for the years 1969–1970 and 1970–1971 and to list faculty salaries and benefits for each faculty member teaching during 1970–71.

The analysis of curriculum offerings is based upon courses actually taught in 1970–71, not those listed in the catalog or in the registrar's office which did not materialize due to limited enrollment or alternate-year registration. Faculty were included only if they were actually present on the campus during the 1970–71 year; faculty on leave or sabbatical were not counted.

Some discrepancies inevitably occur between the figures an individual college gathered about itself and those presented in this report. These differences result, in part, from our difficulty in deciphering data supplied by some colleges, but perhaps in greater part from the systems used to group selective information. The subject classifications used in this analysis, for example, do not always correspond to college departments. Subject classifications are based upon the most common distribution present among liberal arts colleges and according to the United States Office of Education classification system. When colleges submitted data based on their administrative organization, faculty time, student time, and costs were divided and allocated according to the subject classification exhibited in this chapter. Each college in the study can regroup the subjects presented here into any departmental organization and have an accurate picture by department, although comparison with other institutions would not be possible.

All participating colleges did not respond to every item, nor was every category in the project appropriate to every institution. Many subjects were not offered at all schools, particularly in the professional area. All comparative tables, however, are drawn from individual tables prepared for each institution, and all data have been reworked to present a national profile useful to a wider range of colleges.

Tables in this chapter list only the subjects offered by most colleges examined. Totals for subject areas include all subjects offered and taken in the colleges, even though the specific discipline is not listed. In the natural sciences physical geography is left out; in the social sciences geography, anthropology and archeology are eliminated; in the humanities linguistics, Latin, Russian, Portuguese,

Italian, and Chinese are missing; and in the professional area agriculture, engineering, library science, and medical technology are not included.

The tables divide colleges into three categories, to reflect differences related to size and to enable other colleges to compare themselves more accurately. Colleges are ranged in groups under 500 students, 500 to 1000, and over 1000, which more appropriately might be classified as 1001–1500, since only one college exceeded 1500 students. The credit hour is the common denominator for most of the analyses. The credit hour is not the only or the best unit of measure that could be applied, since it leaves out many other aspects of the educational process. But the credit hour is the most universal, the most transferable, and consequently the easiest unit to use for comparative purposes. An institution undertaking a cost study is strongly urged to develop units of measure for other aspects of the teaching-learning process—such aspects as committee assignments, advising of students, and extent or rate of learning—which the credit hour does not touch.

The eleven colleges on the quarter system are included in the master tables but are adjusted to fit the semester pattern. When they were assessed initially, they were separated in order that they might compare themselves with each other. These institutions have been merged with the larger group in order to eliminate an inordinate number of statistical tables and to give a broader picture of private higher education.

Several special problems of methodology were encountered which need explanation at the outset. Physical education was lifted out of the analyses because it was difficult to determine the ways in which colleges perceived this activity. Colleges occasionally merged physical education costs with intercollegiate athletic costs. Faculty in physical education sometimes served as intercollegiate coaches, coordinated intramural programs, or held other administrative positions such as athletic director, dean of students, recruiter, or admissions officer. It was difficult to determine whether credit was given for physical education courses and whether physical education was an integral part of one of the academic divisions or relegated to the periphery.

Applied music also presented a special problem. All applied

music was credited on faculty load in the ratio of one hour of credit for each student per term, and courses were counted the way the institution listed them. In applied music this makes quite a difference; for example, colleges that list strings, percussion, woodwinds, and brass have considerably fewer different courses in applied music than those listing courses titled by each instrument in an orchestra.

Laboratories in the sciences also were credited on the basis of three hours of lecture and laboratory equals four hours of faculty load. For students, laboratories and music lessons were given the credit established by the college. All January interterms were counted as part of the offerings of the second semester. This was an arbitrary decision as were some of the other judgments listed above. In order to compare institutions an arbitrary decision was required which could not be defended in a given institution. Individual colleges can adopt the judgments made here and feel reasonably secure, since every effort was made to choose the allocation method commonly accepted among the largest number of institutions.

Cost of Curricula

Although this section deals with only a limited number of the possible variables in the academic program of any institution, the feeling existed among institutions participating in the project that the most significant variables were treated—with the possible exception of the distribution of students in courses outside their major department, the knowledge of which is important in planning and has a great effect upon the allocation of cost to a particular department. A department may not be responsible for the program or the students for which it is charged. This kind of analysis is called an induced course load matrix.

Student enrollment. Most colleges want to be larger than they are. The answer to the question "How large should we be?" has an immediate bearing on the quality of the education offered and certainly has a great deal to do with the cost. The final chapter of this volume discusses the problems of institutional size and relationship of size to cost.

The colleges in this study varied considerably in full-time-equivalent enrollment for the 1970–71 academic year, ranging from

151 to 2183 students. Twenty-one institutions enrolled fewer than 500 students; forty institutions ranged between 500 and 1000; five institutions exceeded 1000, but only one of these institutions had more than 1500 students. Enrollment for all institutions averaged 653.

Student enrollment by subject is a basic variable with which this study began. A number of the tables, particularly the distribution of student time by class size and by subject offering, show the student credit hours and the student enrollment in various subject areas of the institutions. Enrollment distributed within each subject at different colleges portrays the diversity of institutional electives and requirements taken by students.

The mean average ratio of faculty to students was $1:15.5$ for all colleges, although it ranged from $1:10.5$ to $1:24.4$. Faculty-student ratio is directly related to institutional size ($a = .05$). Colleges under 500 had an average ratio of $1:13.8$; colleges 500 to 1000 had a ratio of $1:16.4$; and colleges over 1000 had a ratio of $1:17.3$. A minimum ratio of faculty to students may be established in order for colleges to offer what is generally conceived to be a broad liberal arts curriculum. Once established, this ratio need not be contracted as the institutions grow. These variations in faculty-student ratios mean great differences in the unit cost of instruction, and there is little reliable evidence that the quality of learning rises with a decline in the number of students per instructor.

Caution must be exercised, however. Simply increasing the ratio of students per faculty member may not reduce costs meaningfully if the method is to remove junior-level faculty, who receive the lowest pay and have been at the college the least amount of time. Differences in the cost of junior and senior faculty cause considerable variations in the costs of expanded or contracted student-faculty ratios.

Credit-hour distribution. The credit hours taught and taken are the second and third critical variables analyzed. Table 1 details the percentage of offerings by subject area. Credit-hour figures represent the total for all courses, including sections and repeated courses. The top half of the table pictures the distribution of course credit hours taught; the bottom half shows the courses taken by students in credit hours. Time spent by faculty in the social sciences,

Table 1.
Percentage of Offerings by Subject Area—1970-71

Subject Area	Under 500		500-1000		Over 1000		All Colleges	
	Mean	Range	Mean	Range	Mean	Range	Mean	Range
CREDIT HOURS TAUGHT								
Natural Sci.	17.6	4.9–25.9	18	3.3–27.8	16	15.2–18.1	17.6	3.3–27.8
Social Sci.	20.2	12.2–33.1	19.5	5.6–32.3	17.5	11.9–22.7	19.3	5.6–33.1
Humanities	45.4	24.3–71.1	44.3	23.4–73.5	32.7	14.7–50	42.7	14.7–73.5
Professional	16.8	0–39.2	18.2	5.9–43	33.8	13.9–46.8	20.4	0–46.8
CREDIT HOURS TAKEN								
Natural Sci.	15.8	6.5–27.5	17.1	6.8–33.9	17.1	15.4–21.4	16.9	6.5–33.9
Social Sci.	24.8	13.8–50.4	26.3	3.9–39	23.9	16.9–32.2	25.6	3.9–50.4
Humanities	44.2	30.9–68.6	41.2	23.9–66.5	32.3	14 –47.1	40.3	14 –68.6
Professional	15.2	0–27.2	15.4	5.1–39.2	26.7	17.3–47.3	17.2	0–47.3

measured in credit hours taught, exceeded the time spent by faculty in the natural sciences by about 10 percent. In contrast, credit hours taken by students in the social sciences exceeded by 40 percent those taken in the natural sciences. Whereas the humanities represented about 43 percent of the credit hours taught, they represented only 40 percent of the credit hours taken. Time spent teaching professional subjects was greater than the time students spent taking them. In both hours taught and hours taken, the proportion of credit hours in the professional area increases as the size of the institution increases—indicating that as colleges grow larger, a larger proportion of student time is spent in professional subjects and a smaller proportion in traditional liberal arts programs. The large difference between hours taken and hours taught in the social sciences reflects larger classes and greater popularity, particularly since institutions have very few requirements in the social sciences compared to the humanities, and indicates that the social sciences underwrite some of the costs of the professional subjects and the humanities.

Compared with the 1962 data (Hungate and Meeth, 1964, p. 17), in which considerably fewer hours were taken in relationship to the number taught in the social sciences in twenty-five selective liberal arts colleges, the rate of growth of the social sciences is increasing. Since 1962, in the relationship between credit hours taught and taken, the humanities have declined in direct ratio to the increase in the professional subjects. These smaller, less selective colleges may have more stringent humanities requirements; if these requirements were relaxed, students would probably go into areas of greater interest to them, such as the social sciences or professional subjects. Comparison between credit hours taught and credit hours taken does not reveal any great decline in traditional liberal arts study. The decline in enrollments in the humanities as institutional size increases, however, does lead to the suspicion that if the humanities were not required to the extent that they presently are, enrollments would be even lower. Apparently the humanities as traditionally conceived are on the decline even in the colleges which are their strongest advocates. Other tables that follow portray this factor in even greater detail.

Some interesting changes in distribution of course credit hours have occurred in the intervening years since the 1962 study. In both the 1962 and the present study, the humanities constitute the largest area of instruction, though in the selective institutions this was only 36.3 percent as opposed to 42.7 percent in the nonselective colleges. Social science represented 28.4 percent in the selective institutions in 1962, opposed to 19.3 percent in the 1970–71 group. The natural sciences were also larger, accumulating 22.6 percent of the credit hours taught, as opposed to 17.6 percent in the present analysis. Professional subjects, representing only 12.7 percent in 1962, now reflect 20.4 percent of the offerings. The social sciences have not been as available to students in the less selective institutions with high religious and humanistic requirements; and professional subjects, with their greater vocational emphasis, have been on the increase.

Analysis of certain subject areas within individual institutions is obscured by the collective table. When institutions are compared individually, great differences become evident. A college, for instance, that devotes 49 percent of its total educational program to the humanities and only 10 percent to professional subjects is a totally different kind of institution from a college that devotes only 23 percent of its total program to the humanities and 25 percent to professional subjects. Neither distribution is "good" or "bad." If colleges have achieved a particular balance in their program through conscious application of their aims and philosophy, then the distribution accurately reflects their ability to pay for it. If, however, they have drifted with the social or educational tide, they ought to take a critical look at their present distribution and their probable direction of development in terms of institutional objectives, types of students to be served, and resources available to provide for that constituency in the future.

Just as course credit hour means something different to different institutions, student credit hour (what a student must do to gain credit toward graduation) also differs from college to college and even within one institution from department to department. What a student must do to gain one hour of credit in English, for example, may be quite different from what he must do in music, psychology, or chemistry. Some of the more important variations resulting from local differences in interpretation of student credit hour depend upon the number of weeks in a semester, the number of times a course meets in a week, the number of minutes in each session, the amount of work required to gain the credit, and whether or not course hours or credit hours are used in the determination.

The mean student credit-hour load in these sixty-six colleges ranges from 9.1 to 19.2, averaging 14.6. Student credit-hour load is not a factor of institutional size and does not vary significantly except on the basis of the number of credit hours required for graduation, the limits placed upon the number of credit hours the student may take per term, and the amount of money students who take fewer or more courses than a specified range must pay per credit hour. These three factors bear directly on the number and variety of courses that students elect and condition the average student credit-hour load in each institution. For instance, in those colleges that allow a credit-hour range unaccompanied by a tuition increase, students commonly accumulate more credits than are required for graduation or graduate in fewer than eight semesters. This practice may be desirable, but two questions of educational propriety can be asked: "Is it better for students to study more broadly among the curricular offerings or concentrate in fewer subjects?" and "Is it appropriate for students who take fewer hours to subsidize those who choose to move more rapidly through the program?" Questions of institutional economy also can be asked in the same regard.

In 1961–62, the natural sciences accounted for 21 percent, the social sciences 34 percent, the humanities 34 percent, and professional subjects 11 percent of the average student load. As in the present study, students in 1962 spent less time in the humanities than did faculty and spent considerably more in the social sciences than did faculty. The natural sciences stayed approximately the same, but faculty offerings in the professional area exceeded student responses.

When institutions are viewed individually in terms of the distribution of student credit hours taken, the relative emphasis on various subject-matter areas studied by students is revealed. The distribution of instruction which students in one college received is quite different from what students in another institution got and calls into serious question the universal nature of so-called liberal education. If students in one college spend 47 percent of their time in professional subjects and in another institution spend 48 percent of their time in the humanities (the balance being distributed among the other areas in both cases), they are getting quite a different liberal arts program. Similar diversity exists among most of the institutions studied. A liberal arts education is by no means universally understood by faculty or students in selective or nonselective private liberal arts colleges, and what is nationally recognized as a liberal arts degree may be radically different from college to college.

Majors. Both the number of different majors and the distribution of students among the various majors bear careful consideration. In these small colleges the number of different majors per institution ranges from 4 to 26 and averages 14.5. The range of majors in all sixty-six colleges is also the range of the group enrolling fewer than 500 students. The number of majors offered is not related to the size of the college. Twenty-six percent of the schools have a major for every other faculty member, and 65 percent have a major for fewer than every third faculty member teaching in 1970–71. If a college enrolls fewer than 1000 students and has twenty-five possible majors, that college has an average distribution of forty students per major, or approximately five to ten graduates a year. Taking into account the uneven distribution among majors and the larger number of freshmen and sophomores who never finish points up the small classes and consequent high costs which must exist when so many majors are allowed.

The natural and social sciences each account for an average of 3.5 majors; humanities, with five majors, has the most; and the professional area has the least, 2.8. Half the colleges studied have no physical education major, and seven have no natural science major. How many majors does a liberal arts college need? Probably not as many as the faculty think and certainly no more than one major for every three or four full-time-equivalent faculty members actually teaching.

An analysis of majors declared by students is not highly reliable for a single college. Since a declared major is not always the final choice and since each college contains a large group of students who have not declared a major, the distribution becomes doubtful. A better estimate for planning within an institution may be a linear view of the number of students graduated over a five-year period in each of the majors, accompanied by a statement of the declaration of major of all the students within the institution. A comparison of these two documents would help establish or challenge the validity of the statement of declaration.

On the other hand, a statement of declared majors is very valuable for portraying national trends. The validity question raised in a single institution becomes less important when all colleges are taken together. Subject fields in which students across the country exhibit the greatest and the least interest, for example, can be helpful to an individual college planning new majors or phasing out existing ones.

The largest major in the natural sciences is biology, except in the institutions enrolling fewer than 500 students, in which a group major in physical science is the largest. The second largest is mathematics. The smallest is physics, averaging only 6.3 students per college; and chemistry is the next smallest, averaging only 9.3 students.

In the social sciences psychology and history tie for largest, except in the smallest colleges, where the group major in social science is largest. Sociology is next, with political science the smallest and economics the next smallest. In the humanities English is the largest major, again except where the group major is largest in the small colleges. English is closely followed by religion and music, both representative of the strong church relationship of the institutions under study. Any one of the foreign languages can be classified as the smallest, with philosophy next. Traditional subjects in the humanities, such as philosophy and foreign language, are not regarded as important areas of study at the present time in these liberal arts institutions.

Among the professional subjects education is the largest major, averaging 100 students per college in those institutions enrolling fewer than 500 students. Nursing is next, averaging 60 students where it exists. It is difficult to portray the smallest major in the professional area, since many different subjects are classified together.

Table 2 documents the percentage distribution of declared majors by subject area in the sixty-six colleges in 1970–71. The percent of majors increases in the natural sciences as institutions increase in size. This factor may have to do with the availability of equipment and facilities and the consequent quality of instruction available in larger institutions. It also may be a factor of institutional emphasis and interest. The social sciences, humanities, and professional subjects tend to be constant across institutional size in the percent of majors. In the institutions enrolling more than 1000 students, business is a much larger professional major (averaging 180) than is education; as institutions grow, reliance upon education as a primary professional subject apparently decreases and students move into areas with a better placement potential.

Courses taught. Different courses taught is one of the most critical variables in the assessment of curriculum in small colleges. Table 3 details the total number of different courses offered by subject in 1970–71. No sections and no courses repeated in both semesters are included. Every listing in this table constitutes a different course title and subject matter. The number of different courses offered by a college should be determined by the number of courses necessary for a student major, for contextual requirements servicing other departments, and for general education and some electives. Since each of these factors is fairly constant from college to college, the number of courses offered in a subject should also be fairly constant. Interestingly, however, the average number of different courses taught increases with total enrollment, indicating a positive correlation between the variety of instruction and the size of the colleges.

Questions can be raised immediately as to why institutional size should make any difference in the variety of offerings necessary to provide an adequate liberal arts college major in institutions which vary in size no more than 1200 students at the most. Yet size is the only factor apparently related to any breakdown of the courses taught. One explanation is that the number of faculty, which is also related to institutional size, is a determinant of the number of different courses offered. Faculty work hard to provide each faculty member with a variety of courses which he in particular wishes to teach. This usually means an increase in the number of offerings. As the number of faculty expand, the number of offerings will expand. There is no pedagogical principle to support this inevitability.

Many colleges with small enrollments offer twice as many different courses as do colleges twice their size. Table 4 details

Table 2.
Percentage of Declared Majors in Subject Area—1970–71

	Under 500		500–1000		Over 1000		All Colleges	
	Mean	Range	Mean	Range	Mean	Range	Mean	Range
Natural Sci.	9	0–18.5	12.4	0–39.9	15	6.4–19.1	12	0–39.9
Social Sci.	22.9	0–46.8	23.6	3.6–53.8	22.3	13.3–35.6	23.4	0–53.8
Humanities	26.5	2.8–86.4	27.1	7.2–70.9	26	6.9–41.4	26.8	2.8–86.4
Professional	41.6	0–69.1	36.9	0–77.5	36.7	15.8–65.5	37.8	0–77.5

Table 3.
NUMBER OF DIFFERENT COURSES OFFERED IN SELECTED SUBJECTS[a]—1970–71

Subjects	Under 500		500–1000		Over 1000		All Colleges	
	Mean	Range	Mean	Range	Mean	Range	Mean	Range
Natural Sciences								
Biology	9.4	1– 20	11.2	3– 21	12.4	2– 20	10.8	1– 21
Chemistry	6.9	1– 13	9.9	3– 18	11.8	9– 15	9.3	1– 18
Geology	3	1– 6	2.9	1– 9	1	—	2.7	1– 9
Mathematics	8.9	1– 19	14.1	3– 23	16	11– 23	12.6	1– 23
Natural Sci.	4.5	1– 10	2.4	1– 6	—	—	2.8	1– 10
Physical Sci.	3	1– 6	2.9	1– 7	4.7	1– 11	3.2	1– 11
Physics	4.4	2– 9	5.6	1– 14	9	5– 11	5.8	1– 14
Total	26.6	5– 64	42.5	4– 71	52.2	39– 69	38.2	4– 71
Social Sciences								
Economics	3.8	1– 8	7.1	1– 22	11.8	6– 15	6.9	1– 22
History	12.4	3– 23	14.6	7– 25	19.2	12– 28	14.3	3– 28
Political Sci.	3.3	1– 11	5.8	1– 18	9.6	3– 13	5.4	1– 18
Psychology	8.1	3– 14	10.2	1– 24	15.2	8– 23	10	1– 24
Social Sci.	4.1	1– 11	7.4	1– 13	2.7	2– 4	5.4	1– 13
Sociology	6.6	1– 14	11.6	1– 30	10.2	5– 15	10	1– 30
Total	31.9	17– 62	46.2	14–104	69.8	45– 93	43.4	14–104
Humanities								
Art	10.9	1– 23	13	1– 39	18	1– 34	12.8	1– 39
Drama	5.3	1– 9	8.8	3– 21	14	13– 15	8.1	1– 21

English	14.6	5– 37	19.3	10– 36	26.8	17– 38	5– 38	18.4
French	5.6	2– 20	8.1	2– 23	7.4	3– 12	2– 23	7.4
German	5	2– 11	5.8	2– 12	4.6	2– 9	2– 12	5.5
Greek	3.7	2– 7	4.5	2– 9	4.5	3– 6	2– 9	4.3
Humanities	4.8	1– 17	4.4	1– 24	3.5	2– 5	1– 24	4.4
Latin	4	—	2.8	1– 5	5	4– 6	1– 6	3.4
Music	20.6	2– 86	28.9	1– 68	35.4	2– 59	1– 86	26.8
Philosophy	6.1	2– 13	6.6	2– 15	9	3– 14	2– 15	6.6
Religion	16.8	2– 66	13	1– 28	20	4– 36	1– 66	14.6
Spanish	6.8	2– 19	8.1	2– 17	8.4	4– 15	2– 19	7.6
Speech	4.9	1– 14	8.7	2– 23	11.3	5– 23	1– 23	7.8
Total	84.7	37–234	114.5	48–202	144.8	63–226	37–234	107.3
Professional								
Accounting	8	—	5	2– 11	12	10– 16	2– 16	8.1
Business	11.9	1– 26	13.8	4– 42	15.8	3– 26	1– 42	13.6
Education	12.2	1– 37	15.9	3– 32	18.6	5– 32	1– 37	15
Home Ec.	11	7– 20	16	6– 23	17	13– 21	6– 23	14.9
Total	25.4	2– 75	39.3	10– 98	84.2	50–146	2–146	38.7
Subtotal	166.2	73–386	242.5	150–424	351	295–438	73–438	226.5
Physical Ed.	19.2	5– 86	24.6	5– 47	27	3– 42	3– 86	23.3
Grand Total	181.7	73–470	266	162–470	378	317–474	73–474	247.6

*Excludes all sections and courses repeated in both terms. Totals for each subject area (e.g., Natural Science), subtotals, and grand totals include all subjects taught at all colleges even though they are not listed by subject.

selected subjects in six institutions. Why could College B, with four
more students than College A, offer a ten-course major in biology
while College A offered seventeen? Why did the same situation
prevail in chemistry and mathematics? How could College E offer

Table 4.
COURSES OFFERED IN SELECTED SUBJECTS
IN SIX COLLEGES—1970–71

College Code	A	B	C	D	E	F
Enrollment	469	473	628	643	789	804
Natural Sciences						
Biology	17	10	8	9	7	11
Chemistry	12	5	9	9	9	10
Mathematics	16	6	14	11	13	14
Social Sciences						
History	17	8	16	9	13	19
Psychology	11	5	15	5	7	16
Sociology	14	4	14	9	3	15
Humanities						
English	22	15	15	12	17	21
Music	10	6	25	29	26	18
Religion	9	10	8	12	4	8
Professional						
Business	18	11	13	—	14	13
Education	37	13	16	8	10	17
Other	149	46	153	57	78	152
Total	332	139	306	170	201	314

a program in history with thirteen courses, while College F offered
nineteen? Even more dramatically, College E offered seven courses
in psychology, and College F offered sixteen. Each of the pairs of
institutions was radically different in psychology and sociology offerings, suggesting that these programs are much more in flux than
some of the humanities. In English, however, College A offered
twenty-two courses and College B offered fifteen. In business College
B offered eleven and College A offered eighteen. Education in each
of the pairs of institutions of similar size is as dramatically different

as is psychology. The total number of courses offered in the pairs comes close to being 40 percent different.

Although this study does not pretend to explain or justify these variations, it does raise serious questions concerning the size of some departmental programs. Inevitably the larger programs mean small classes, heavy teaching loads, and, in the absence of large endowments, low salaries. The end result is a gradual deterioration of the quality of the educational program. Since these institutions exactly parallel the problem found in the 1962 study of twenty-five selective institutions (Hungate and Meeth, 1964), course prolifera-tion seems to be universal among private institutions. Many have overextended their curricular offerings in some departments; unless they reduce their offerings or increase their enrollments without increasing faculty, they cannot operate economically nor can they raise the quality of instruction they do give.

Several curriculum writers and economists in American education have suggested that a small college need offer only two or three courses beyond the number it requires for a student major in any given year. Thus, if the department of English requires thirty hours for a major, it ought to offer no more than forty hours— excluding sections, general education courses not counted toward the major, and contextual requirements for other departments. Since a full faculty load is normally twenty-four hours, or eight courses in a year, two faculty members could adequately teach all the different courses required for a major in any institution under 1500 students. Additional faculty may be required for sections and general educa-tion courses as enrollments increase, but it is difficult to rationalize a broader program of different courses of study. Since the student will take no more than thirty to forty hours, and since that number could be expanded by offering different courses in alternate years, the private college should not mimic the university and try to cover all aspects of every subject it offers.

The problem of expanded offerings is further compounded when Table 3 is related to number of full-time-equivalent faculty per subject in each institution. In the natural sciences teachers in smaller colleges must be generalists, able to teach various subjects well, while in the larger institutions teachers can be specialists, teach-ing one or two parts of a subject field. Hence, many colleges must find teaching assignments that neither require the professor to teach every aspect of the subject nor leave him bored by too limited a teaching assignment. This dilemma, plus power plays and the willingness of faculty to work beyond the normal load required of them, has caused the expansion of curriculum to the point that administrators find themselves forced to add faculty in order to cover courses listed in the catalog.

Colleges in the project also were asked to indicate courses not taught but listed in their catalog for two years. The two-year span was requested to avoid inclusion of any alternate-year courses. The result of this survey (Table 5) shows that no institution among the sixty-six taught all courses listed in the catalog and that at least one course in every area was not taught in some institution. The number of courses not offered ranged from 3 (which is insignificant and could occur very easily) to 124 (which is one fourth to one half of the offerings of most of the institutions analyzed). An average of thirty-nine courses listed in the catalogs of these institutions were not taught for two years. These colleges have an ethical problem in that the catalog is perceived by parents and students as a learning contract describing what the institution provides for the tuition paid. When courses are not offered as advertised, the college is in an ethical, if not a legal, dilemma. It is understandable to find courses in a single year's catalog which may not be offered and are covered by an addendum, but for them to appear two consecutive years seems untenable.

Faculty. In these sixty-six colleges the number of faculty for the first session of 1970–71 ranged from 12.4 in the smallest institution to 107.5 in the largest. The size of the faculty is positively related to the size of the institution. Not only the total number of faculty but also the number of faculty in every major subject area increases as enrollment increases.

Although faculty size is related to institutional size, faculty work load, commonly called *teaching load measured in credit hours,* does not increase or decrease in relationship to institutional size. Teaching load likewise is not related to class size.

Table 6 outlines the distribution of teaching load by percent. America can be credited with calling the vocation of professional teachers a "load." Twenty-three percent of the faculty in these in-

Table 5.
COURSES LISTED BUT NOT OFFERED
IN SELECTED SUBJECTS—1969–1971

	All Colleges	
	Mean	Range
Natural Sciences		
Biology	3.1	1– 10
Chemistry	2.8	1– 8
Geology	2	1– 4
Mathematics	3.1	1– 9
Physical Sci.	3.9	1– 12
Physics	2.6	1– 9
Total	7.6	1– 34
Social Sciences		
Economics	2.2	1– 7
History	4.2	1– 15
Political Sci.	2.3	1– 6
Psychology	3.1	1– 9
Social Sci.	2.5	1– 10
Sociology	2.8	1– 6
Total	8.7	1– 28
Humanities		
Art	2	1– 5
Drama	2.3	1– 6
English	3.1	1– 12
French	2.2	1– 6
German	2.7	1– 6
Greek	2.9	1– 9
Latin	6.8	2– 10
Music	4.7	1– 19
Philosophy	2.2	1– 7
Religion	4.8	1– 22
Spanish	3.1	1– 11
Speech	3	1– 9
Total	17	1– 61
Professional		
Accounting	2.4	1– 5
Business	2.8	1– 12
Education	3.6	1– 13
Home Ec.	2.5	1– 9
Total	5.8	1– 32
Grand Total	38.9	3–124

stitutions taught fewer than seven hours in the fall term of 1970–71; only 13 percent taught 15 hours or more in the same semester.

Faculty in the sixty-six institutions taught an average credit-hour load ranging from 6.8 to 14.5, with a mean average of 11.2 credit hours. This wide range of teaching loads for full-time faculty members in some measure indicates different institutional policies with respect to how many hours per week faculty members should be in the classroom. But other factors also play a part in determining these figures. The teaching load of some faculty members, for instance, is lower because they also have administrative duties; the teaching load of others is raised because they have temporarily assumed the teaching responsibilities of faculty on leave. Unexpected registration may increase teaching assignments. The desire for research, the need for extra income, the love of teaching, and poor or good teaching ability also affect teaching loads. Careful administrative supervision is needed to ensure that some members of the teaching staff are not excessively burdened while others carry an inequitably light load.

A subject-division analysis of teaching load reveals that faculty in the natural sciences taught the lightest load, while those in the humanities and the social sciences taught the heaviest. This distribution may be weighted by the way in which laboratories are counted, but the question may be raised whether institutional differences in teaching responsibilities rest upon any objective studies of the effect of instruction on learning or indeed on any rational ground whatever. Certainly some of the institutions which turn out broadly educated citizens as well as alumni acceptable to graduate schools have above-average teaching loads. More extensive analysis of teaching load is necessary to determine whether there is any relationship between the credit hours a faculty member carries and the quality of his teaching and whether there is a point beyond which the credit hours that a faculty member carries result in diminished learning among students.

Another way of measuring faculty work load is to assemble the total number of student credit hours produced by each faculty member in an academic year. This figure, commonly called *productivity,* averaged 471 credit hours per instructor among the sixty-six institutions. Average productivity per faculty member ranged from 225 through 770 credit hours per year. Productivity is related

Table 6.
DISTRIBUTION OF TEACHING LOAD BY PERCENT—FALL 1970

Credit Hours Taught	All Colleges	
	Mean	Range
Under 7	23.1	2.5–54
7– 8.9	12.3	0–28
9–10.9	16.7	2.1–54
11–12.9	26.5	2.6–63.3
13–14.9	8.2	0–33
15–16.9	7.9	0–35
17–18.9	1.9	0–13
19 and over	3.4	0–21.1

to institutional size ($a = .05$). The larger the institution, the harder faculty members work in terms of numbers of students taught. Althought they may not have to teach as many different courses in a large college, the number of persons taught is greater—resulting in an equalization of work load among faculty in smaller and larger private colleges.

In return for their teaching in 1970–71, faculty members received an average of $9369 and an additional $746 worth of benefits, for a total average compensation of $10,115. Although productivity is related to institutional size, cash salary is not related to faculty work load. Benefits do increase as institutional size increases, but not sufficiently to cause total faculty compensation to be significantly related to institutional size.

Since faculty compensation tends to be the largest single item in the educational and general budget of small colleges, it is important to look at the ratio between faculty salary and all other educational expenditures (called *overhead*). This figure, representing the funds in addition to faculty salaries necessary to keep a teacher in the classroom, could be called *educational expenditures other than faculty salaries*. However named, it is the only figure that can show the relationship between faculty salary, which is perhaps the most critical expenditure in the educational program, and all other expenses—such as plant maintenance, departmental expenditures, general administration, student services, and the library—which enhance and supplement the work of the classroom teacher.

For every dollar spent on faculty salary, an average of $1.85 was spent for all other educational areas in 1970–71. This overhead ratio on faculty salary ranges from 70 cents to $3.50, indicating the great differences in allocation of institutional resources between faculty and other aspects of the educational program. The overhead ratio is not related to institutional size but is more a factor of institutional management.

Class size. In recent years there has been much discussion of the relative merits of small and large classes. Most research has been related to empirical measures of cognition, with very little concern about student or faculty attitudes. Nevertheless, what research has been done has not produced an optimum class size for most efficient learning. Classes can be too small, so small that student interaction is not possible; but it has yet to be demonstrated that information retrieval is reduced by a very large class. Particularly crucial to the amount of learning that students acquire is the faculty member's own attitude toward the size of class he teaches. If he is comfortable with a large class, students tend to learn more than if he is uncomfortable lecturing to a large group.

The sixty-six colleges in this study differed markedly in the average size of their classes. They ranged from a mean average of 9.9 to 34.7, with an average class size for all institutions of 20.1 students.

There is a marked relationship between size of the institution and the size of classes ($a = .01$). Average class size in this study increased up to an enrollment of about 850, at which point the relationship leveled off. In the 1962 study (Hungate and Meeth, 1964) average class size increased up to an enrollment of 2000 before the relationship leveled off. In any case, the relationship points out a particularly acute problem in colleges under 800: to provide even a modest curricular offering, these colleges will necessarily have a number of small classes and suffer an obvious economic penalty. To provide sufficient courses for few students, some colleges must maintain proportionately larger faculties than their sister institutions with larger enrollments and larger classes.

Table 7 distinguishes the percentage of teacher and student credit hours in the sixty-six institutions by class size. The figures in this table dramatically demonstrate the differences between the amounts of time students and teachers spent in small and large classes. Classes with one to five students accounted for an average of 18.3 percent of the teacher credit hours (or time) but only 2.5 percent of the student credit hours. That is, more than 18 percent of the faculty time was spent instructing 2.5 percent of the students. In classes with an enrollment between six and ten, roughly 16 percent of the faculty time was spent instructing 6 percent of the students. Grouping these together, over one third of the faculty time in colleges under 2000 was spent instructing less than one tenth of the students. This practice is obviously very expensive and, when not a part of a conscious effort, should be seriously reviewed.

Some colleges have small classes by design. However, visits to more than thirty of these institutions elicited little conclusive evidence that any of the colleges in this study deliberately choose small classes. Instead, as a result of the number of faculty employed and the different courses offered, they are forced to operate at a high cost and appear to be wasting their limited economic resources. Many of these institutions probably could increase the average size of their classes by one to five students without affecting the quality of the program; they could also reduce the number of faculty needed and consequently reduce the cost of instruction.

Table 7 shows that institutions also differ widely in the percentage of large classes they offer. Classes ranging in size from forty-one to over fifty students absorbed nearly one third of student time and were taught by approximately 10 percent of the faculty. Balancing faculty time in small classes against faculty time in large classes, and the same for student time, results in a reasonably equitable mean distribution. Economical large classes in basic informational courses can be offered without deterioration in educational quality. Even though seminars, tutorials, and small discussion groups have value, they do account for large expenditures and ought to be justified by demonstrable results in effective learning.

The aim of an analysis of class size is not to urge institutions toward the median, which is approximately twenty students per class, but instead to make a conscious analysis of the range of class

Table 7.
Distribution of Staff and Student Time by Class Size—1970–71

PERCENTAGE OF TEACHER CREDIT HOURS

Class Size	Under 500		500–1000		Over 1000		All Colleges	
	Mean	Range	Mean	Range	Mean	Range	Mean	Range
1– 5	20.6	5 –36	18.6	7.5–34	14	3 –33.3	18.3	3 –36
6–10	21.2	7 –33.7	15	7.6–21.1	11.5	8 –15	15.7	7 –33.7
11–15	16	9 –21	14.8	8.9–23.9	13.5	11.4–15.5	14.9	8.9–23.9
16–20	10.5	4 –19	12	6 –22	12.9	9 –18	11.8	4 –22
21–25	9.7	2.5–24	10.9	4 –19	12.9	10 –17	11	2.5–24
26–30	6.9	.8–15	8.3	2.9–19.4	11	6.5–19	8.4	.8–19.4
31–35	3.9	0–10	5.1	1 – 9.7	8.7	5 –13	5.4	0–13
36–40	3.5	0– 9	3.7	.6– 8.5	6.8	1 – 9.5	4.2	0– 9.5
41–45	2.5	0– 7	3	.8– 7.6	2.3	1 – 4.8	2.8	0– 7.6
46–50	1.2	0– 8.3	1.6	0– 4.4	1.7	1.5– 3	1.5	0– 8.3
Over 50	4	0–14.1	7	1 –20	4.7	2.9–10	6	0–20

PERCENTAGE OF STUDENT CREDIT HOURS

Class Size	Under 500		500–1000		Over 1000		All Colleges	
	Mean	Range	Mean	Range	Mean	Range	Mean	Range
1– 5	3.4	1 – 7	2.6	.9– 6.7	1.6	1 – 3.6	2.5	.9– 7
6–10	9.5	2 –23	5.6	2.6– 9.2	4.3	3 – 5.5	6.1	2 –23
11–15	11.6	6 –27	9.2	4.5–16.7	7.9	7 – 8.8	9.4	4.5–27
16–20	10.4	4.2–20.9	10.2	3.1–21	10.8	6 –14	10.3	3.1–21
21–25	12.5	3.6–27	11.8	5.1–21	13.6	8.5–17	12.4	3.6–27
26–30	10.9	1.7–28	11	2.2–26	14.2	9.5–24	11.5	1.7–28
31–35	7.2	0–19	8.1	2 –14.7	13.2	9.3–19	8.8	0–19
36–40	7.6	0–15	6.7	1 –15.1	11.7	2 –17.4	7.7	0–17.4
41–45	5.9	0–16	6	1 –13.4	4.4	1 – 9.7	5.7	0–16
46–50	3.4	0– 9	3.5	0– 9	3.7	3.5– 7	3.5	0– 9
Over 50	17.6	0–52.7	25.3	3 –59.6	14.6	8 –27	22.1	0–59.6

size in terms of faculty and student time and to balance small classes against large classes in order to achieve an economical distribution. The economic balance of small and large classes can be specified by a relationship. When the proportions of faculty and student time in classes under eleven are reversed in classes over forty, optimum economy seems to be reached. Thus, if 33 percent of faculty time and 10 percent of student time are spent in classes under eleven, then 10 percent of faculty time and 33 percent of student time should be spent in classes over forty. (This relationship can be expressed in a formula which says that optimum economy is a function of the concurrence of converse proportions of faculty and student effort devoted to polar levels of class size: $E_o = f[(x\%_f, y\%_s)_a + (y\%_f, x\%_s)_z]$.)

Comparison of averages. Table 8 lists the institutional averages for some of the variables discussed in preceding sections and three of the variables to be discussed in the next section. This table shows the relationship of the various factors to institutional size and serves as a summary for this section of the chapter. These figures indicate a few trends but do not make any evaluations; they simply describe the 1970–71 behavior of a group of private liberal arts colleges. Items listed on Table 8 are the basic data needed for any cost analysis of the academic program. The fact that these institutions substantiate the findings of the 1962 study of quality and cost of liberal arts programs (Hungate and Meeth, 1964) adds evidence that the colleges in these studies are typical of most other liberal arts colleges. Hence, these data are significant for all of private higher education.

Current Operations

The critical economic aspects of curricula, in addition to those already considered, include the cost per credit hours, cost per student, and the percent of income paid by tuition and fees. Beyond the immediate cost of curricula, several relationships exist which will be explored in depth and the major variables in curriculum brought together in a cost-relationship formula.

Cost. One way of viewing current operational costs of the curriculum is to assess the cost per student credit hour—based either

Table 8.
Comparison of Averages in Sixty-six Colleges—1970–71

Item	Under 500		500–1000		Over 1000		All Colleges	
	Mean	Range	Mean	Range	Mean	Range	Mean	Range
FTE faculty	27.1	12.4– 44.5	46	22.3– 71	82	58.1–107.5	42. 7	12.4–107.5
Average class size	17.7	9.9– 28.6	21	12.2– 34.7	22. 1	17.5– 26	20. 1	9.9– 34.7
Average teaching load	12	9.1– 14.5	10.8	6.8– 14.3	11. 6	10.8–13	11. 2	6.8– 14.5
Average faculty productivity (in student credit hours)	408.6	224.9–535.3	494.2	348.3–770	542. 4	439.9–749.9	470. 8	224.9–770
Average student credit-hour load (1st sem.)	14.6	9.3– 16.8	14.6	9.1– 19.2	14. 8	13.3– 15.9	14. 6	9.1– 19.2
Faculty-student ratio (1st sem.)	13.3	10.5– 17.4	16.4	11.3– 24.4	17. 3	14.2– 19.1	15. 5	10.5– 24.4
Average FTE faculty cash salary	$9267	$7265–11,633	$9503	$7,094–13,416	$8715	$7369–10,343	$9369	$7094–13,416
Average FTE faculty benefits	$576	$80–1052	$812	$199–1551	$854	$692–1161	$746	$80–1551
Average FTE total faculty compensation	$9843	$7686–12,101	$10,315	$7713–13,911	$9569	$8061–11,505	$10,115	$7686–13,911
Overhead ratio	1.8	.7– 3.5	1.9	.89– 2.9	1.82	1.3– 2.5	1.85	.7– 3.5
Average cost per student	$1944	$1360–2,930	$1848	$1169–2534	$1564	$1249–1979	$1857	$1169–2930
Average income per student	$1185	$691–1679	$1409	$457–2052	$1324	$1061–1541	$1330	$457–2052
Total educational expense	$692,480	$397,375 to 1,040,974	$1,363,386	$743,594 to 2,447,108	$2,209,789	$1,553,253 to 2,725,763	$1,211,740	$397,375 to 2,725,763
Total educational income	$435,791	$161,821 to 717,630	$999,370	$266,317 to 1,730,954	$1,871,804	$1,476,671 to 2,315,903	$884,401	$161,821 to 2,315,903
Percent of expenditure borne by tuition & fees[a]	57.2	38.7– 85	70.4	33 – 97.8	79. 3	66.7– 89.1	66. 8	33 – 97.8

[a] Excludes unfunded scholarships.

on total faculty compensation or on faculty compensation plus departmental expenditures, which comprise the total direct costs of the educational program. Tables 9 and 10 portray these breakdowns for the sixty-six institutions. Faculty cost per student credit hour depends upon the total compensation paid the faculty member, which in turn depends on his rank and length of service and on what it cost to hire him originally. It also depends on the number of students taught in the subject. The larger the number of students taught, the lower the cost per credit hour.

Faculty cost per credit hour in all institutions in the study averaged $20.11. This average is not related to institutional size and varied only 81 cents among the three size categories. The mean obscures the very large range. Average faculty salary cost per credit hour taught ranged from $11.51 to $29, which indicates that some colleges are spending more than twice as much for every credit hour of instruction than other institutions in the same study. Since faculty cost per credit hour is not related to institutional size, it would seem that the cost, theoretically at least, could be as constant as the mean for each size category. This is not at all the case. Some institutions are paying small salaries to faculty members who are working very hard and producing more than 500 student credit hours per year. Other institutions are paying high salaries to faculty who teach few students in the course of a year, resulting in a very high faculty cost per student credit hour. On the other hand, some institutions in the study are clearly more efficient than the others and do balance pay for work produced.

Physical education is the most expensive subject in the institutions but lies outside the four areas discussed because it is not a reliable figure. Among the subject areas, natural science is the most expensive, at $23.39 per student credit hour; and social science is the least expensive, at $14.86 per student credit hour. Chemistry is the most expensive subject within the natural sciences, closely followed by physics. In all divisions the general education subjects are least expensive, since they usually are taken by all students in the college.

In the social sciences, political science leads all other subjects, followed by economics as the next most expensive. Psychology and sociology are quite inexpensive, as is history. In fact, all the

Table 9.
Faculty Cost per Student Credit Hour—1970-71

Subject	Under 500 Mean	Under 500 Range	500–1000 Mean	500–1000 Range	Over 1000 Mean	Over 1000 Range	All Colleges Mean	All Colleges Range
Natural Sciences								
Biology	$19.93	$ 9.00– 45.55	$21.60	$12.23– 45.36	$18.39	$14.52– 24.16	$20.88	$ 9.00– 45.55
Chemistry	29.57	12.16– 85.70	39.72	14.04– 98.93	40.53	27.28– 66.68	38.35	12.16– 98.93
Geology	16.47	12.63– 24.57	17.21	4.39– 45.48	—	—	17.01	4.39– 45.48
Mathematics	20.62	13.07– 40.94	21.40	11.90– 50.18	16.94	15.09– 18.86	20.34	11.90– 50.18
Natural Sci.	34.44	17.99– 46.30	7.43	3.20–107.81	—	—	9.65	3.20–107.81
Physical Sci.	20.91	11.94–103.23	12.96	4.48– 30.80	13.98	5.70– 15.34	14.19	4.48–103.23
Physics	23.51	7.77– 91.42	36.94	13.41–126.55	30.52	22.53– 52.03	34.18	7.77–126.55
Total	21.81	11.59– 37.14	23.41	3.20– 40.72	21.92	18.87– 28.56	23.39	3.20– 40.72
Social Sciences								
Economics	20.20	11.53– 26.64	20.12	4.08– 53.50	17.76	12.21– 26.23	19.25	4.08– 53.50
History	17.54	7.54– 94.65	13.48	1.98– 40.41	17.85	11.04– 28.61	14.78	1.98– 94.65
Political Sci.	24.68	4.38–166.67	22.80	3.26– 64.50	21.18	16.70– 28.73	22.58	3.26–166.67
Psychology	12.93	3.37– 21.66	12.34	4.60– 22.61	11.72	6.42– 15.78	12.35	3.37– 22.61
Social Sci.	10.95	5.70–256.00	11.84	4.26– 38.87	11.51	3.46– 14.38	11.55	3.46–256.00
Sociology	11.33	3.42– 34.15	13.67	5.60– 56.46	17.00	9.74– 20.26	13.79	3.42– 56.46
Total	16.24	5.64– 21.90	14.16	5.71– 22.29	16.56	12.26– 20.89	14.86	5.64– 22.29
Humanities								
Art	24.36	8.33– 50.88	24.23	4.45– 67.50	26.21	16.01– 41.14	24.56	4.45– 67.50
Drama	34.17	19.04– 76.13	28.66	10.40– 63.99	43.34	29.30– 51.96	31.72	10.40– 76.13

English	18.09	7.14– 34.51	18.30	9.57– 68.72	19.34	13.30– 24.57	18.41	7.14– 68.72
French	34.75	14.04–101.20	33.64	9.25–126.67	28.74	17.76– 49.03	33.29	9.25–126.67
German	28.91	23.82–133.33	33.37	7.86–120.64	17.93	13.16– 28.48	29.42	7.86–133.33
Greek	41.52	13.51–158.61	34.24	13.01– 70.11	66.17	43.06–214.75	37.08	13.01–214.75
Humanities	15.41	9.94–148.77	10.50	3.80– 61.73	11.37	8.87– 20.08	11.67	3.80–148.77
Latin	—	—	43.20	20.83– 61.72	74.29	39.23–148.56	68.07	20.83–148.56
Music	53.79	35.43– 85.74	38.45	14.21– 83.66	51.75	19.57–117.94	41.69	14.21–117.94
Philosophy	19.38	1.00– 74.47	16.62	6.22– 90.85	22.04	11.21– 27.78	17.70	1.00– 90.85
Religion	15.88	10.53– 54.93	13.87	5.48– 59.00	35.86	29.67– 38.15	14.82	5.48– 59.00
Spanish	27.45	13.88– 72.72	24.87	11.11– 55.71	25.65	6.07– 61.65	25.46	6.07– 72.72
Speech	23.66	2.29– 39.99	21.76	3.29–119.39	19.02	6.04– 23.06	21.66	2.29–119.39
Total	21.19	16.83– 31.86	20.75	12.27– 36.63	25.96	18.37– 35.10	21.41	12.27– 36.63
Professional								
Accounting	$21.81	—	$20.34	$12.77– 45.01	$14.33	$ 8.39– 35.63	$16.11	$ 8.39– 45.01
Business	24.85	11.97–47.07	21.44	6.01– 75.15	13.35	10.84– 19.21	19.69	6.01– 75.15
Education	19.92	7.84– 83.39	19.70	4.47– 50.55	20.63	19.23– 24.58	19.84	4.47– 83.39
Home Ec.	18.63	18.45– 18.81	28.34	20.17– 37.47	36.97	—	28.03	18.45– 37.47
Engineering	—	—	24.48	20.37– 51.85	15.75	15.75– 15.79	18.50	15.75– 51.85
Total	20.54	12.17– 83.39	20.93	9.85– 38.31	16.98	16.46– 22.96	20.19	9.85– 83.39
Subtotal	20.04	15.93– 28.65	19.49	11.62– 28.21	20.82	16.22– 26.39	19.77	11.62– 28.65
Physical Ed.	24.89	11.95– 43.00	30.70	19.75– 65.00	19.37	14.21– 58.71	27.47	11.95– 65.00
Grand Total	20.31	16.58– 29.00	19.93	11.51– 28.68	20.74	16.10– 27.18	20.11	11.51– 29.00

social sciences are economical in relationship to other subjects in the institution, suggesting that expansion in the social sciences would be less expensive than in other areas.

In the humanities, foreign languages are quite expensive. Music, however, is the most expensive major subject in liberal arts colleges, costing an average of $41.69 per hour among all institutions but ranging as high as $148 per hour. Religion, required at many of the colleges in this study, is the least expensive subject outside the general education program.

In the professional area, home economics is the most expensive and accounting the least expensive subject. Education and business are very close together. Too few colleges have programs in journalism, nursing, or engineering to warrant any comparison of cost for faculty in these areas.

The range of faculty cost per student credit hour for the major disciplines is perhaps more significant than the mean, demonstrating the tremendous difference in what colleges pay faculty and require of students. Certainly many questions can be raised about the necessity for the great range in cost. Regardless of institutional size, beyond a certain minimum cost the difference should flatten out considerably; but it does not. Could not colleges with high faculty cost per student credit hour in a particular subject area reduce the number of faculty and increase class size and thereby reduce the faculty cost per credit hour? Would such an undertaking jeopardize the quality of instruction or the amount of learning acquired by students? These two qualitative questions are the most critical when analyses of cost are made. Chapter Five probes them in depth.

Departmental expenditures added to faculty compensation produces the total direct cost per student credit hour. Table 10 takes into account, in addition to faculty compensation, all expenses for equipment, student assistance, supplies, communications, and faculty departmental benefits such as travel allowances to professional meetings. This table parallels the faculty-cost table throughout and reveals that departmental costs in the humanities and natural sciences add an average cost of $2 per hour, the social sciences add $1 per hour, and the professional subjects add $3 to faculty costs. Direct

Table 10.
Direct Cost per Student Credit Hour by Subject Area—1970–71

	Under 500 (14 colleges)		500–1000 (27 colleges)		Over 1000 (4 colleges)		All Colleges (45 colleges)	
	Mean	Range	Mean	Range	Mean	Range	Mean	Range
Natural Sci.	$24.40	$12.26–60.55	$26.24	$ 3.20–41.31	$24.25	$21.23–32.77	$25.54	$ 3.20–60.55
Social Sci.	17.41	10.11–25.41	15.37	5.87–23.04	17.79	13.01–21.52	15.93	5.87–25.41
Humanities	23.64	17.40–39.77	22.63	13.95–37.98	27.25	19.38–36.92	23.46	13.85–39.77
Professional	25.75	13.91–83.39	24.54	13.89–41.90	19.84	17.05–27.91	23.26	13.79–83.39
Subtotal	21.14	16.90–28.89	20.97	12.52–29.88	22.20	18.53–28.02	21.23	12.52–29.88
Physical Ed.	29.72	16.23–56.43	32.35	20.15–66.32	22.96	15.81–76.47	29.75	15.81–76.47
Grand Total	22.25	17.67–29.40	22.04	12.49–30.58	22.23	18.38–29.21	22.10	12.49–30.58

costs per institution are roughly $2 per credit hour more than faculty costs for 1970–71.

Another way to deal with current operational costs beyond the credit hour is to look at costs per student. In the sixty-six colleges the average income from student tuition and fees was $1330 and the average cost per student was $1857, indicating that the average institution had to pick up a little over $500 per student enrolled. The range of income varied from $457 to $2052. Some of the colleges in this study charge very little, and no institution exceeds the tuition cost of the selective private colleges. The range of the cost to educate these students varied from $1169 to $2930. This range is as great as the range in income and represents a considerable disparity, which is probably not reflected in the quality of the product turned out by some institutions at the extreme ends of the range.

The average cost per student in each institution was determined by dividing the total current institutional expenditure for the 1970–71 academic year by the average full-time-equivalent student enrollment. The expenditures, drawn from institutional financial reports and audits, included all items customarily classified as educational and general: general administration, student services, public services and information, general instruction, departmental research, libraries, plant operation and maintenance. Excluded were expenditures for organized research and for programs not included in the regular academic year, such as summer and evening study if they were treated separately, and for auxiliary debt service depreciation and unusual capital outlay. Research was included under educational expenditures because in these institutions the only research conducted was internally supported. Almost no contractual research involving another type of expenditure was undertaken.

These expenditure-per-student figures raise questions about the economy of the institutions studied. Are students in the institution that spends nearly $3000 on each graduate receiving twice as good an education as those in the institution that spends only $1500? Since tuition fees make up the largest percentage of income in the institutions with the highest charges, are some students unnecessarily overcharged and others of limited means actually deprived of a higher education by high fees that are not related to the quality of instruction? What is the effect of high expenditures on the kinds of students the college attracts?

The great difference between institutional income from student tuition and fees and the cost to educate the same student results in the colleges' receiving an average of 66.8 percent of the educational cost from the student. This percent of expenditure paid by tuition and fees excludes unfunded scholarships. Money that a college gives to students as scholarship aid from its general operating funds and for which it has no outside support is called *unfunded scholarship aid*. Student expenditure paid by students ranges from 33 percent to 97.8 percent. In other words, in some institutions students are paying only one third of the cost of their education while in others they are paying almost the total amount. As other sections of this volume reveal, cost per student does not seem to be related to other aspects of the educational program. The percent of expenditure borne by tuition and fees increases as institutional size increases; larger institutions acquire a larger percentage of their income from students than do very small colleges.

There is no optimum figure in the literature of higher education to suggest what percentage of their educational costs students should be paying. The percent of cost that students pay needs to be balanced between fluctuations in student enrollment and fluctuations in the economy. Thus, a healthy percentage would range somewhere between 65 and 80 percent of income to the institution from student fees. If the figure is lower than 65 percent, the institution would suffer radically from a tight economy, particularly if it had a small endowment and had to depend upon gifts and grants and government funding when these resources were more limited than normal. Likewise, 80 percent seems to be maximum; otherwise, an institution is in financial jeopardy if students do not materialize. A decrease in enrollment means that the college must gear itself for either drastic cutbacks or great increases in outside funding after commitments have already been made for the bulk of the potential income.

Cost relationships. Over twenty different cost relationships, both statistically significant and insignificant, were examined and the most meaningful reported. Some of these relationships were expected, but others were contrary to general economic concepts reported in earlier years.

That cost per student is significantly ($a = .02$) related to income per student was one of the expected relationships. Colleges which spend more per student pass that cost on to the student in higher charges. If increased cost per student equaled increased quality of learning or satisfaction, such a practice might be justified; but, as Chapter Five points out, there is great doubt that increased cost *does* equal increased quality.

The larger the college, the greater is the proportion of its income derived from students ($a = .01$), another anticipated outcome. Not so evident, however, is the fact that cost per student is unrelated to the percent of expenditure borne by tuition. Although cost per student and income per student are related, the percent that the student pays of that cost is a ratio not related to cost per student.

Although class size is directly related to institutional size, it is not at all related to cost per student. The colleges collectively gain no apparent saving by increasing class size. A single school may make great gains by increasing class size and reducing faculty, but collectively other factors outweigh that economy.

Just as very little else is related to cost, the number of different majors offered by these colleges is not related to cost per student. In individual colleges, of course, the addition of even one major can make quite a cost difference if new faculty, equipment, or facilities are required. But in the aggregate, no matter how many majors there are, cost is not affected.

Faculty productivity, represented by the average student credit hours taught per faculty member, should markedly affect expenditures per student. In other words, colleges whose faculty teach a large number of credit hours should spend less per student than institutions whose faculty teach a small number of credit hours. This relationship was barely significant ($a = .05$), indicating that colleges with high faculty productivity generally have a lower per-student cost.

The most meaningful relationship of all—a relationship that helps to explain some of the others—is that cost per student is not related to institutional size. Although the Carnegie Commission (1972b, p. 164) and others have suggested otherwise, larger colleges apparently do not have lower costs. The schools in this study spend every dollar they can find and more without regard, collectively, for an optimum cost per student in relationship to size. Colleges which seek to increase enrollment as a way of balancing the budget predicate their behavior on the assumption that increased enrollment reduces per-student cost. This assumption is false for this group of colleges, although it may be true for individual institutions. Increased enrollments without other changes are part of the economic problem of small colleges, not the solution.

The relationship between faculty compensation and per-student cost was examined. As faculty compensation increases, do student costs also increase? In the 1962 study (Hungate and Meeth, 1964), we found a significant relationship between average salaries and per-student expenditures: when salaries went up, cost per-student went up. This relationship no longer holds true. In the sixty-six colleges studied in 1970–71, faculty salaries are not statistically related to the cost per student. This finding suggests that the other areas of expenditure determined by administrators exercise greater control over total cost per student.

A number of factors appear to be directly related to institutional size. Number of faculty, average class size, average faculty productivity, average student load, faculty-student ratio, and percent of income from tuition and fees—all go up as institutional size increases. The fact that these six factors increase with size reveals that faculty work harder as size increases but do not earn more for their effort, whereas students also work harder as size increases and are charged more for it. These six characteristics which relate to size suggest that management is to some extent at least cognizant of these relationships. Almost all the significant variables are related to size in the direction in which the literature of higher education predicts they ought to be. The problem, however, is that the relationships are not necessarily valid for any one institution. In some colleges the relationships are in balance, but in a number of others no relationships exist among these factors at all.

Cost formula. The critical curricular variables are related to each other and to the cost of instruction in all institutions. These variables can be examined most clearly through the use of a relational formula developed by Harris (1962, p. 519). This formula demonstrates the relationship of variables over which faculty and administrators have control to the total cost of the educational program. As the formula shows, the administration and faculty can alter any one of these variables and by so doing change the others and the cost of instruction within the institution.

The formula is composed of a series of letters symbolizing each of the variables in curricular cost analysis:

1. Number of students (N) *times* semester student load in credit hours (L) *equals* total student credit hours.
2. Average class size (C) *times* average semester credit hours taught by teachers (F) *equals* average student credit hours taught by each teacher.
3. Total semester student credit hours *divided by* average credit hours taught by teachers *equals* number of teachers.
4. Number of teachers *times* average academic-year salary of teacher (S) *equals* total teachers' salaries.
5. Total year's expenditures *less* teacher's salaries *equals* overhead on teachers' salaries.
6. Overhead expressed as a relative of salary *equals* overhead *divided by* salaries (0). (Overhead stands for all costs other than salary.)
7. Thus: $\frac{(NL}{CF)} S (1 + 0) =$ cost of instruction.

College K enrolls 722 students, who carry an average load of 16.5 credit hours. These figures are divided by an average class size of 22.3 times an average faculty credit-hour load of 12. When these four figures are multiplied and divided, they equal the number of faculty necessary to teach in that institution. Many faculty do not realize that the number of full-time-equivalent persons necessary to meet an institution's commitments is based entirely on these four factors. The number of faculty *times* the average faculty salary *times* 1 *plus* the overhead rate *equals* the cost of instruction:

$$\frac{(722 \times 16.5)}{(22.3 \times 12)} \times \$8868 (1 + 1.4) = \$947,527.$$

Suppose that College K increases enrollment 20 percent; the students, however, choose to take the same number of hours, and the faculty insist that class size is as large as can be managed and that they will not work any harder. Then those four variables multiplied and divided would require the institution to hire more faculty in order to meet the increased enrollment and would consequently raise the cost of instruction by many thousands of dollars. Conversely, if the faculty agree that they can indeed teach 20 percent more students in their courses without noticing the difference, particularly since the institution has so many small classes, and none of the other variables are changed, the number of faculty needed to teach in that college goes down and the cost of instruction goes down by several thousands of dollars. Similar changes are documented for each of the variables.

If enrollment (N) is increased 20 percent:

$$\frac{(886 \times 16.5)}{(22.3 \times 12)} \times \$8868 \ (1 + 1.17) = \$1,026,275.$$

If enrollment (N) is decreased 20 percent:

$$\frac{(578 \times 16.5)}{(22.3 \times 12)} \times \$8868 \ (1 + 1.75) = \$868,779.$$

If student load (L) is increased 20 percent:

$$\frac{(722 \times 19.8)}{(22.3 \times 12)} \times \$8868 \ (1 + 1.17) = \$1,026,452.$$

If student load (L) is decreased 20 percent:

$$\frac{(722 \times 13.2)}{(22.3 \times 12)} \times \$8868 \ (1 + 1.75) = \$868,513.$$

If class size (C) is increased 20 percent:

$$\frac{(722 \times 16.5)}{(26.8 \times 12)} \times \$8868 \ (1 + 1.68) = \$881,194.$$

If class size (C) is decreased 20 percent:

$$\frac{(722 \times 16.5)}{(17.8 \times 12)} \times \$8868 \ (1 + 1.12) = \$1,047,292.$$

If average teaching load (F) is increased 20 percent:

$$\frac{(722 \times 16.5)}{(22.3 \times 14.4)} \times \$8868 \ (1 + 1.68) = \$881,726.$$

If average teaching load (F) is decreased 20 percent:

$$\frac{(722 \times 16.5)}{(22.3 \times 9.6)} \times \$8868 \ (1 + 1.12) = \$1,046,228.$$

Rarely is an institution free to manipulate only one of these variables at a time. In most colleges the variables move in sets, and increases or decreases in faculty number cannot be achieved as easily as the formula implies. But the formula does suggest that every college administrator and every faculty member should be cognizant of these relationships that have such direct bearings upon salaries, the cost of instruction, and how hard people have to work for what they are paid.

Unfortunately, very little change has occurred in the factors analyzed in this chapter since a comparable study was undertaken in 1962. The conclusion to that study is still the most appropriate conclusion which can be envisioned: "No college can be effectively administered in the absence of the kinds of information presented in this chapter. Without it decisions must be uninformed, casual, and sometimes unrelated to the overall purposes for which a college exists. Moreover, though some types of economy may be educationally undesirable, a more discriminating use of the limited resources available to most institutions must be made if their quality is to be maintained at a competititive level. Unless one makes the assumption that financial resources will in the future be unlimited, inefficient and wasteful management must inevitably result in poorly paid teachers, inadequate buildings, impoverished libraries, and a consequent lowering of institutional quality. This undesirable prospect can be avoided only by the immediate inauguration of a program of professionally manned institutional research and the establishment of some agency within the institution charged with the responsibility for long-range planning, for it is obvious from the results of this study that even after the facts are available and understood by all concerned, some years will be required to accomplish the needed changes in policy and practice" (Hungate and Meeth, 1964, p. 36).

Chapter III

᠄᠄᠄᠄᠄᠄

Income and Expenditure

Sources of institutional income and distribution of institutional expenditures are two of the most critical factors of viability. The distribution of income and expenditure reflects administrative and faculty commitments. Colleges with large student services, for example, are quite different from colleges with none or very few. The distribution of income and expenditure also reflects institutional "givens." Colleges with high plant costs usually live in old buildings on large tracts of land. No college today dares let the distribution of finances occur randomly.

Fifty-six colleges submitted audits and financial profiles for 1970–71. These profiles were carefully analyzed to ensure that each contained the same data for the same categories in all institutions. From these data tables were compiled which detail total institutional income and expenditure and take a closer look at income and expenditure in the educational and general category. These tables should be helpful to colleges that wish to compare their income and expenditure distribution with the fifty-six colleges analyzed in 1970–71. Caution should be exercised, however, since these tables represent only one year of operation and since the distribution by no means reflects the most desired distribution of income and expenditure expressed by numerous higher educational economists in the last decade.

The items and categories in this chapter correspond to those in *The Sixty College Study of Income and Expenditures—A Second Look* (1957–58), except that two categories—intercollegiate athletics and other educational operations—are here listed separately, rather than subsumed under auxiliary enterprises and education and general, respectively, in order to highlight how very little these colleges are concerned with either category. Data from this sample of small nonselective colleges in the country is thirteen years newer than the second *Sixty College Study* and therefore should be of greater help to persons concerned with the distribution of finances in private liberal arts colleges.

These income and expenditure data are not accurate profiles of these institutions except for the one year 1970–71. To get a genuinely accurate measure, it would be necessary to include at least a three-year period to reflect the changes in institutional financing. A college in 1970–71, for example, could receive a very large gift for operation and receive nothing at all for 1971–72 and 1972–73. Thus, a three-year distribution of income would reflect considerably different percentages than for the year in which the large grant was received. Likewise, colleges could have unusual expenditures or postpone expenditures for 1970–71, which would not reflect the financial behavior of the institution over three years.

As mentioned, then, institutions using these tables to compare their own income and expenditure should be guided by the fact that they do represent only one year, even though they are a cross section of fifty-six different institutions of reasonably homogeneous purpose and structure.

Table 11 summarizes total current income by percentage for 1970–71 for all institutions which presented usable data. As noted in Chapter Two, the institutions are divided into three categories: under 500 students, 500–1000, and over 1000. The over-1000 column includes only five colleges and is not as reliable as the other two. Grouped together, however, the total college statement represents institutions under 1500 in the private sector of American higher education.

These small colleges receive 70 percent of their income in the educational and general category, 25.2 percent for auxiliaries, 4.4 percent in student aid, only .1 percent in other educational operations, and only .3 percent in intercollegiate athletics. Clearly, other educational operations (a category including specialized programs funded outside the institution) are not a viable part of the operation

Table 11.

TOTAL CURRENT INCOME BY PERCENTAGE
IN FIFTY-SIX COLLEGES—1970–71

Enrollment	Under 500	500–1000	Over 1000	All Colleges
Educational and general	72.6	68.1	75.6	70.0
Auxiliary enterprises	23.6	26.4	21.9	25.2
Student aid	3.6	5.1	2.2	4.4
Other educational operations	.0	.1	.0	.1
Intercollegiate athletics	.0	.3	.3	.3
Total Current Income	100	100	100	100

of the nonselective small college. In like manner, intercollegiate athletics does not even produce income in institutions under 500 and, in the colleges between 500 and 1500, produces considerably less than 1 percent of all the income. None of the categories of total current income appear to be affected by institutional size.

Table 12.

TOTAL CURRENT EXPENDITURES BY PERCENTAGE
IN FIFTY-SIX COLLEGES—1970-71

				All
Enrollment	*Under 500*	*500-1000*	*Over 1000*	*Colleges*
Educational and general	64.2	66.0	68.9	66.0
Auxiliary enterprises	21.1	22.2	21.5	21.9
Student aid	7.3	7.9	5.8	7.5
Other educational operations	.0	.0	.0	.0
Intercollegiate athletics	.7	1.1	1.4	1.1
Debt service	6.7	2.8	2.5	3.5
Total Current Expenditures	100	100	100	100

Table 12 summarizes total expenditures by percentage for the same group of institutions in 1970-71. Educational and general expenditure accounted for 66 percent of total expenditures, which averaged 4 percent less than income. Auxiliary enterprises expended 21.9 percent of all dollars, which averaged 3.3 percent less than income. Student aid accounted for 7.5 percent of all expenditures, which was 3.1 percent more than income, resulting in a fairly sizable amount of unfunded scholarship monies. Other educational operations were not significant enough to be listed. Intercollegiate athletics accounted for 1.1 percent of expenditure, and debt service accounted for 3.5 percent.

Educational and general expenditures are related to institutional size. The percentage of dollars spent for educational and general activities increases as institutional size increases, suggesting that larger institutions with a greater amount of income are able to distribute their expenditures more broadly. In particular, debt service, which is related to institutional size in reverse order, is less a problem for larger institutions. Small colleges with limited resources have tended to pile up a large debt-service expenditure, which reduces the funds available for educational and general activities and ties the institutions to a more rigid distribution pattern. In like manner, the very small colleges pay a larger proportion of income for student aid in order to keep the students coming, which restricts the percentage of funds allotted for educational and general expenses. The percentage relationship of institutional size to the categories educational and general and debt service does not necessarily correlate with dollar amounts but with the way in which the colleges were able to distribute expenditures among the various categories.

Table 13 details educational and general income for the fifty-six colleges in 1970–71. Seventy percent of income came from student fees. As institutional size increases, the percentage of income from student fees also increases, partly because the larger institutions charge students a larger portion of the cost of their education.

Government appropriations accounted for 2 percent of the educational and general income. As colleges increase in size, the percentage of government appropriations decreases. According to this analysis, small colleges are much more dependent upon government allocations than are larger institutions and will be in greater jeopardy should these appropriations be reduced or eliminated. Fortunately, however, the extent of reliance upon government appropriations in the educational and general area, in this group of institutions at least, is not great and seems to be at a level from which the institutions could recover if 2 percent of their income in the educational and general area were removed.

Three percent of the educational and general income came from endowment. These colleges have very limited endowments. They rely heavily upon large church contributions—in the form of outright grants, pledges from denominations or individual churches, or, in the case of Roman Catholic institutions, through contributed services. These church ties constitute an endowment in the minds of many of the administrators; but church ties are no substitute for an

Table 13.

EDUCATIONAL AND GENERAL INCOME BY PERCENTAGE
IN FIFTY-SIX COLLEGES—1970-71

Enrollment	Under 500	500-1000	Over 1000	All Colleges
Student fees	59.1	72.3	79.7	70.5
Government appropriations	2.8	2.0	.7	2.0
Endowment	1.6	3.9	.4	3.0
Gifts and grants	23.0	13.7	8.8	15.0
Contributed services	6.5	3.3	5.1	4.2
Sponsored Research	.4	.2	.0	.2
Other separately budgeted research	.0	.0	.0	.0
Other sponsored programs	2.5	.9	1.8	1.3
Organized activities	.5	.7	.2	.6
Miscellaneous	3.6	3.1	3.1	3.2
Total Educational and General Income	100	100	100	100

independent, stable source of income upon which the institution can rely from year to year.

Gifts and grants accounted for 15 percent of the income. The amounts here reduce as institutional size increases—again because very large contributions, ranging between $100,000 and $200,000, are received by the very small, evangelical, Protestant colleges; these colleges, as Table 13 shows, received 23 percent of their educational income from gifts and grants. In more selective institutions the endowment and gifts and grants categories would be balanced in a different fashion. Contributed services accounted for 4.2 percent of the educational income and is normally a figure representative only of Roman Catholic institutions.

These small colleges participate in virtually no research, receiving .2 percent of their educational income from sponsored research and none from separately budgeted research. Faculty in the nonselective small colleges do not write many proposals and consequently do not receive many grants for research activities which they can carry on in conjunction with their teaching responsibilities.

Other sponsored programs—summer school, evening session, field trips, church conferences, and similar educational activities— accounted for 1.3 percent of the educational income. This is a very small part of the potential income that these institutions might collect if they were imaginative in developing ways of expanding their normal offerings to other groups of people with whom they have some affinity: churches, older women in the community, veterans, and other persons with similar convictions who are not now served by traditional liberal arts offerings.

Organized activities (a category that includes all enterprises operated by educational departments primarily for professional training of students—such enterprises as choir concerts and field trips) accounted for .6 percent of income. Miscellaneous income (which includes current fund investments, rent from educational buildings, salvage value of equipment sold, parking fees, and conferences) accounted for 3.2 percent of the educational income. These two categories are quite open-ended and, consequently, contain many different specific items of income from the college. No great reliance should be placed on the percentages in the two categories except that, in both instances, the figures are quite small.

Table 14 outlines the educational and general expenditures for the fifty-six colleges in 1970–71. This table varies from the *Sixty College Study* and other national guidelines in that staff and faculty benefits are divided to allow for cost accounting of the direct instructional costs. Development also is lifted out of the general institutional category in order to highlight this activity. The relationship of expenditure and income in the development office is examined in Chapter Four.

Instructional salaries accounted for 37.5 percent of the educational expenditure in these institutions, and instructional supplies and expenses accounted for 6 percent. As institutional size increases, so does the percentage distribution for instructional supplies and expenses—suggesting that the larger institutions place more emphasis

Table 14.

EDUCATIONAL AND GENERAL EXPENDITURE BY PERCENTAGE
IN FIFTY-SIX COLLEGES—1970–71

Enrollment	Under 500	500–1000	Over 1000	All Colleges
Instructional salaries	37.2	36.5	42.9	37.5
Instructional supplies and expenses	3.5	6.5	7.1	6.0
Organized activities	.6	.8	1.3	.8
Sponsored research	.4	.2	.7	.3
Other separately budgeted research	.0	.0	.0	.0
Other sponsored programs	2.0	.6	2.1	1.1
Libraries	6.6	5.4	5.7	5.7
Student services	8.7	8.7	9.5	8.8
Plant operation and maintenance	10.5	12.6	10.3	11.8
General administration	12.5	9.5	6.9	9.7
Staff benefits	2.0	2.5	1.9	2.3
Faculty benefits	2.1	2.7	2.9	2.6
Development	5.6	5.8	3.6	5.5
General institutional	8.3	8.4	5.2	7.9
Total Educational and General Expenditure	100	100	100	100

upon adequate supplies and equipment for instruction and are able to allocate more of their resources to this area. Small colleges have traditionally desired to spend 50 percent of all educational dollars on direct instructional activity. When faculty benefits are added to salaries and instructional supplies and expenses, these institutions spent 46.1 percent of available educational dollars on instruction. Most schools still have a long way to go to reach the desired norm. Although the institutions over 1000 did exceed 50 percent of their expenditures for direct instructional activity, the smaller colleges pulled the aggregate total down.

Again, .8 percent was spent on organized activities, .3 percent on sponsored research, and nothing on separately budgeted research. The average expenditures in these categories exceeded average income in the same categories. Expenditures for organized activities also relate to institutional size, increasing as size increases; these figures indicate that larger institutions engage in more activities outside the traditional program than do smaller ones.

Other sponsored programs accounted for 1.1 percent of expenditure. Libraries accounted for 5.7 percent; this figure exceeds the American Library Association standard of at least 5 percent of educational expenses and is less than the more selective liberal arts colleges spent in the 1962 study (Hungate and Meeth, 1964). Student services were a growing part of the educational program through the 1960s, but these small colleges have not acquired as large a student personnel staff or engaged in as many student activities as more selective or larger liberal arts colleges.

Plant operation and maintenance accounted for 11.8 percent of the educational expenditure, which is again down from the 1962 study of twenty-five selective colleges. In small institutions operating with deficits, plant operation is the first item to be curtailed, and an examination of a single year of plant expenses does not portray the picture as it might exist over a three-year period.

General administration accounted for 9.7 percent of the expenditure, which is higher than the percentage spent in 1962. As institutional size increases, the percentage of dollars spent for administration decreases. Colleges under 500 students evidently feel that they must have the same administrative staff as colleges with twice that number of students. The larger the institution, therefore, the greater the likelihood of a smaller percentage of expenditure for administration. This balance may be necessary or deliberate. On the other hand, it may be related to some unsupported assumptions about the number of administrative staff needed for small colleges.

Faculty and staff benefits together accounted for 4.9 percent of expenditure, staff benefits falling slightly below faculty benefits. The National Association of College and University Business Officers does not break this figure apart in its normal accounting procedures; consequently, cost accounting in the instructional areas cannot be completed, since faculty benefits are a part of direct instructional costs. The figure is divided here for the purposes of cost analysis.

Development accounted for 5.5 percent of the total educational expenditure and is responsible for producing, along with the president, all operational and capital income beyond tuition and fees. The development expenditure includes alumni affairs, fund raising, and public information and services.

General institutional expenditure accounted for 7.9 percent of the educational expenditure and is twice the expenditure of the twenty-five colleges in 1962. When development is put back into the general institutional category, the total of 13.4 percent becomes enormous. Small colleges tend to group in this category many items that might be distributed among other more specific accounting lines. This category represents a point of attack for administrators desiring to reduce the indirect cost of the educational program and to increase the distribution of expenses in instructional salaries, equipment, and supplies. Interest payment on operating deficits accounts for far too large a portion of this area.

One of the questions confronting small colleges, particularly those with an annual deficit, is whether the money they pay out in unfunded scholarships is in any way related to that deficit. Unfunded scholarship are those funds used for student aid that are taken from the operating budget of the college, whether from available educational and general income or from auxiliary activities income. Funded scholarships must come from funds set aside by gifts and endowments specifically for student aid. Table 15 outlines the relationship of excess income or expenditure to unfunded scholarship aid.

Forty-five colleges were ranked from the largest deficit to the largest excess income for 1970–71. More than half the institutions in this group had a deficit ranging from more than $600,000 to an insignificant $165. The other institutions had excess incomes ranging from approximately $500 to more than $260,000, four colleges having extra income in excess of $100,000. Student aid income and expenditures were compared, and the difference (expenditures which were greater than income) was listed. A comparison was then made

Table 15.
RELATIONSHIP OF EXCESS INCOME TO UNFUNDED
SCHOLARSHIP AID IN FORTY-FIVE COLLEGES
1970–71

Excess Income over Expenditure	Student Aid Income	Student Aid Expenditure	Difference in Unfunded Scholarships
(672,519)	253,477	435,142	181,665
(316,546)	56,844	106,837	49,993
(261,738)	—	44,286	44,286
(200,110)	55,875	104,473	48,598
(195,846)	82,137	75,757	(6,380)
(175,076)	126,998	166,999	40,001
(145,049)	—	25,272	25,272
(127,092)	6,063	180,759	174,696
(122,141)	—	38,209	38,209
(112,512)	109,924	210,104	100,180
(94,486)	25,773	58,958	33,185
(87,549)	114,172	114,172	0
(61,353)	27,418	149,845	122,427
(49,781)	36,215	46,097	9,882
(43,050)	5,253	16,698	11,445
(32,536)	96,894	110,812	13,918
(32,452)	70,832	170,585	99,753
(29,500)	26,400	34,415	8,015
(25,677)	9,169	35,367	26,198
(19,554)	—	—	0
(17,000)	—	101,461	101,461
(9,000)	112,000	158,000	46,000
(8,470)	5,280	35,786	30,506
(945)	14,500	20,579	6,079
(165)	117,897	111,064	(6,833)
579	371,642	481,556	109,914
5,993	5,609	55,159	49,550
7,017	—	94,296	94,296
16,134	—	77,854	77,854
20,135	77,394	180,992	103,598
28,342	22,777	58,828	36,051
29,977	59,000	59,276	276
48,793	12,715	116,970	104,255
49,170	249,306	345,145	95,835
58,145	55,519	126,133	70,614
58,317	183,268	335,346	152,078
59,424	194,277	295,328	101,051
88,034	16,760	153,347	136,587
88,426	47,834	104,580	56,746
96,957	49,411	151,890	102,479
135,982	131,385	164,693	33,308
189,658	184,433	175,179	(9,254)
240,963	72,100	82,659	10,559
265,285	20,500	99,035	78,535

between deficit and unfunded scholarships or excess income and unfunded scholarships, and no statistical relationship could be found between these two factors.

The lack of relationship suggests that pump priming, as it is commonly known, is still a viable activity for the small college which is short on student aid income. The large amount of unfunded scholarship dollars put out by these institutions does suggest a possible ethical problem in that students who can afford to pay are subsidizing without knowing it those students who cannot afford to pay. Thus, the real cost of their education would be considerably less if such a large percentage of scholarship dollars were not drawn from the operating funds of the institution and came instead from income outside the institution.

Chapter IV

ﰰﰰﰰﰰﰰﰰ

Admissions and Development Costs

At the request of the participating colleges two administrative offices were briefly analyzed. The development office and the recruitment and admissions office were selected for review because they are both critical to institutional survival and they both have good product measures. In development the success of the office is measured by the number of dollars acquired; in the recruitment and admissions office success is measured by the number of students enrolled. Other administrative units have product measures; in the health service, for instance, success depends on the number of people treated, and in the library success depends on the number of materials utilized. Other offices, such as student services, are more difficult to assess because the product measures are not readily agreed upon or are not reliable.

Product measures require norms to give them meaning. The assessments of development and recruitment made in this chapter were designed primarily to produce the beginnings of a normative statement about small nonselective colleges in the United States. These figures are representative of what occurred in 1970–71 alone, and there is no way to know from these data whether that was a representative year or whether both areas suffered significantly in 1970–71.

Development Office

An analysis of income produced by the development office was all that was undertaken. Fifty-eight colleges submitted information for study in 1970–71; the information is reported on Table 16. Any fair analysis of products of the development office in a single college requires at least a three-year look in order to avoid the obvious misrepresentation that can occur in examining a single year. A given college, for example, may receive a large bequest in one year and go for two or three years without receiving any. To assume that the dollars produced in a fat year or a lean year are representative of the total effort of the development staff would be a mistake. This study has data for only one year; but since fifty-eight colleges are represented, and since the mean is very close to the median (not shown on the table) in all the measures, these figures probably represent efforts in these institutions across the years as well as in a single year.

Obviously, the development officers are not solely responsible for fund raising, nor is that their only responsibility. Nevertheless, it is their primary responsibility and is the only area reviewed in this analysis. In other words, even though the president, for instance, often is an important fund raiser and even though faculty and stu-

Table 16.

DEVELOPMENT OFFICE INCOME AND EXPENDITURE IN FIFTY-EIGHT COLLEGES—1970-71

	Under 500		500-1000		Over 1000		All Colleges	
	Mean	Range	Mean	Range	Mean	Range	Mean	Range
Gifts and grants	$165,751	$4,438–294,438	$202,183	$31,854–530,338	$184,954	$ 3,000–314,675	$188,528	$3,000–530,338
Capital income	$115,010	$1,668–517,775	$179,328	$ 1,025–699,116	$179,653	$ 32,909–429,442	$163,635	$1,025–699,116
Total:	$231,810	$4,438–780,696	$354,678	$55,853–767,192	$328,677	$125,000–725,749	$312,187	$4,438–780,696
Expenditures for development[a]	$ 45,691	$1,110–146,502	$ 85,341	$12,376–166,132	$ 70,925	$ 32,796–150,054	$ 70,790	$1,110–166,132
Ratio of income to expenditure[a]	5.2	.2–96.1	4.2	.9–11.9	4.6	3.1–10.6	4.4	.2–96.1
Percent of education and general expenditure for development[a]	5.6	.002–15.7	5.8	.9–10.9	3.6	1.5–10	5.5	.002–15.7

[a] Excludes four colleges reporting no development expenses.

dent service personnel write proposals or design projects which are merely handled by the development staff on their behalf, in this survey the development staff is credited with all the successes and all the failures.

The fifty-eight colleges raised an average of $188,000 in gifts and grants and $163,000 in capital income during 1970–71, for a total of slightly more than $312,000 per institution. Gift and grant income is used entirely for operation of the educational program, but capital income may be expended for buildings, endowment, or major equipment and repairs.

Interestingly, size is no predictor of nontuition income in the colleges examined. The very smallest college is as likely to get a large grant as is the college of 1500. The range of gifts for operation and capital is broad in each of the size categories and reflects no pattern which in any way could suggest that those in the smaller colleges have a disadvantage.

No institution in this study raised more than a combined total of $800,000 for the year, and the maximum for gifts and grants was slightly over $500,000—suggesting that the number of dollars which these institutions can raise successfully is limited. Therefore, college presidents who place an unrealistic burden of expectation upon the development office usually end up disappointed and with a deficit budget. Knowing what colleges across the nation of the same type and size are able to accomplish should help administrators prepare realistic budget projections and goals for the development staff.

The average expenditure for development efforts—which included working with alumni, public relations, and fund raising—was approximately $71,000, but ranged from $1110 to $166,132. Expenditure for development is a relatively insignificant figure. The important figure is the relationship of dollars spent to dollars taken in. If an institution spends $166,000, for example, and takes in $1,000,000, the return for the dollars spent is greater than for the institution that spends only $1000 and takes in $5000. It is a truism to say that it takes money to make money. Far too frequently boards of trustees and presidents have cut development staff dollars in the belief that income will continue at the same rate with fewer staff or program materials. No doubt there is an efficiency level in any development office, but it is equally true that colleges spending larger sums raise more for every dollar they spend.

This factor is revealed in the ratio of income to expenditure. For every dollar spent in development, the average institution brought in $4.40. The range for all institutions is the same as the range for the colleges under 500: from 20 cents to $96.10. One college in the study brought in only 20 cents for every dollar it expended; but another raised $96.10 for every dollar spent, which is extremely unusual for that institution or for any other in this population. Selective independent liberal arts colleges expect to raise approximately eight dollars for every dollar expended for development, but the institutions in this study seem unable to reach this level.

Percent of educational and general expenditure for development averaged 5.5 but ranged from almost nothing to 15.7 percent. Development expenditures are related to other educational expenditures in Chapter Three. Four colleges reported no development expenditure but did have income, indicating that all fund raising was handled through the president's office and that no development staff was hired. But how long can such a situation be maintained without exhausting energies which ought to be divided over a greater range of institutional commitments?

These few figures can guide trustees, administrators, and development directors who are interested in goal setting and minimum potential. Development officers who raised less than one dollar for every dollar expended might better have remained in bed. Institutions that raised more than eight dollars for every dollar expended are exemplary. Assessment of individuals in the development office, however, should not be made on the basis of a single year's effort, and new personnel most certainly should not be expected to produce a record even equal to the average for the small nonselective colleges. Students of development programs say that it takes approximately three years for a development officer to produce anywhere near his capacity and that a person should be given at least that length of time before final assessment is made of his ability to raise dollars for an institution.

The concept of risk capital is an important one for trustees of small colleges to understand. If a college development staff is able to raise four dollars or more for every dollar expended, there should be no limit placed on the number of dollars spent; at the same time, the percent of expenditures for development ought not to rob the instructional programs of the institution. One solution is to set up a risk capital fund large enough to pay the salary of a development officer, including his travel and necessary expenses, for a two- to three-year period. As that person raises funds for the institution, money from his effort is put back into the risk fund; when this fund is restored to its full amount, another person is employed, using that same investment procedure. The staff is continually expanded on the basis of the same risk fund until a full contingent of development officers is established and the saturation point reached for the institution.

By setting aside a specific amount of money for this effort, a college does not drain dollars from the educational program while it is testing out a new individual. The fund provides enough resources to allow a person time to develop his potential and requires that he replace the fund from his efforts as rapidly as possible. In some instances a person will not produce and the capital will be depleted. That is, of course, the nature of a risk fund; but more times than not, it will prove successful if adequate analysis of the task to be performed and the person expected to perform it is made in advance.

Recruitment and Admissions Office

While the study of the recruitment and admissions office is more comprehensive than the assessment of development, it is by no means a complete review. Only major product categories and a few of the leading expenditure items (such as publications and staff) have been reviewed, and no effort has been made to explain the meaning of the figures presented. No one can access from these data why one college is more successful in recruiting students than another. Nor is there any way, on the basis of past experience in the recruitment area, to predict what the success rate will be in the future. Changes occur rapidly, and a considerably more sophisticated analysis would be required to predict the number of staff and the number of dollars necessary to produce any particular number of students even if all environmental factors remained constant.

Recruitment. Tables 17 and 18 portray prospects contacted, applications received, applications approved, and new students enrolled in the fifty colleges responding to this analysis of recruitment and admission practices. The average college contacted over 2500 prospects, but the range among the institutions was from 325 to 9000 student contacts. The average number of contacts is related to institutional size. As colleges grow larger, they tend to have a larger base of contacts from which to draw applications.

This fact suggests something of a problem that the smallest colleges experience. Their base of contacts is small; consequently, the number of prospects is small, and their applications and number of new students remain correspondingly small. The larger the contact base, then, the larger the enrollment. The smallest colleges can refute this truism only by placing a great effort on expanding their base of prospects. This, of course, can be done in a variety of ways—for instance, by urging all faculty and staff and alumni and students to supply names, by following community and junior college leads, and by acquiring leads from local churches and high schools.

The number of applications received is likewise related to institutional size and averages 432 for the fifty colleges. Applications approved are only slightly below, averaging 369, which reveals one aspect of the nonselective nature of the institutions. The number of new students enrolled, like the other factors, is related to institutional size and averages 267 new students. In the colleges under 500 the average new-student enrollment was 205, indicating a very high attrition rate in these colleges.

Table 18 shows ratios of new students enrolled to contacts, applications received, and applications approved; the table then turns the grouping around and looks at applications received and approved and students enrolled in relation to every hundred prospects contacted. The ratio of new students enrolled to contacts is 9.9, which is, of course, the same as the number of new students enrolled for every hundred prospects contacted. Roughly one in ten prospects contacted enrolls in one of these fifty institutions. For every hundred prospects contacted, sixteen apply, indicating a very expensive loss rate between contact and application, and suggesting that the primary area on which these small colleges need to focus their attention is what happens to persons between contact and application.

Table 17.

RECRUITMENT AND ADMISSION FACTORS IN FIFTY COLLEGES—1970–71

Factor	Under 500		500-1000		1000-1500		All Colleges	
	Mean	Range	Mean	Range	Mean	Range	Mean	Range
Prospects contacted	1846	325– 8000	2804	380– 7500	4563	1300– 9000	2627	325– 9000
Applications received	273	150– 471	484	226– 1297	736	600– 900	432	150– 1297
Applications approved	244	150– 558	412	193– 826	595	521– 676	369	150– 826
New students enrolled	205	122– 542	284	152– 449	420	363– 472	267	122– 542
Student fee income	$3080	$750– 4900	$5857	$2260–16,000	$5585	$1500– 9000	$5012	$750–16,000
Admission-recruitment costs (excluding catalog costs)	$30,235	$14,575–62,010	$48,799	$5675–83,187	$63,721	$56,000–74,600	$43,754	$5675–83,187
No. catalogs published	5331	1500–10,800	8240	3500–14,000	7833	3500–14,000	7245	1500–21,645
Catalog costs	$3645	$638–10,280	$4997	$356–10,161	$6238	$2555–10,600	$4631	$356–10,600
Expenditure for all publishing related to recruiting	$6790	$1800– 2100	$8103	$580–15,408	$10,688	$2555–18,031	$7838	$580–21,000
No. professional recruitment-admissions staff	2.3	.85–4	2.8	.25–4.5	3.8	3.75–3.9	2.7	.25–4.5

Table 18.

ADMISSION RATIOS IN FIFTY COLLEGES—1970-71

Item	Under 500	500–1000	1000–1500	All Colleges
Ratio of new students enrolled to total new contacts	9.3	9.9	10.9	9.9
Ratio of new students enrolled to total applications received	1.3	1.7	1.8	1.6
Ratio of new students enrolled to total applications approved	1.2	1.5	1.4	1.4
Number of persons applying for every 100 prospects contacted	13	17	18	16.2
Number of persons accepted for every 100 prospects contacted	12	15	14	14.0
Number of new students enrolled for every 100 prospects contacted	9.3	9.9	10.9	9.9

The prospects may be unrealistic; they may be merely lists of individuals supplied by professional admissions programs, or they may be actual contacts directed toward a specific institution, or they may be a mixture of several possibilities. Nevertheless, concentrating more effort on pursuing prospects and helping them to the point of a full application seems to be the critical area of effort. Once a prospect has applied, he is virtually assured of acceptance, since fourteen out of sixteen are accepted; and the institution is 75 percent assured of an enrollee, since ten out of every fourteen accepted do show. The loss between institutional acceptance and enrollment is significant also, particularly since these prospects have been cultivated extensively.

On the basis of these data, it is possible to project a behavioral formula which reads 100:16:14:10. That is, for every hundred prospects contacted, sixteen apply, fourteen are approved, and ten enroll. Such a formula simply describes behavior as it exists in these institutions and in no way should be used as a goal for colleges. Instead, institutions should try to improve the number of persons who apply and who are enrolled and thus move the relationships in the formula radically upward.

   Publications. A mean average of 7245 catalogs were published by the institutions in this survey. Catalog publication ranged from 1500 to nearly 22,000. The number of catalogs published is not related to institutional size. A number of small colleges published considerably more catalogs than the larger institutions in the population, indicating either a different use for catalogs in the various institutions or an erroneous estimate of the number needed. The average expenditure for catalogs was $4631 but ranged from $356 to $10,600. Total expenditure for catalogs is not a factor of size. A few small colleges are able to get their catalogs published for considerably less than some larger colleges, probably because they include fewer pictures and the size of the catalog is smaller. Since almost all institutions list courses in their catalogs, small schools with many fewer offerings need many fewer pages. But in general small schools pay as much as large schools. Catalogs averaged 65 cents each in these institutions. Cost per catalog is not related to size, suggesting that neither size of catalog nor number published rises sufficiently above minimum publishing costs to afford a price saving.

   Publishing catalogs is an established custom of liberal arts colleges but one which certainly can be challenged in terms of today's market needs. Most experts in recruitment and admissions tell colleges that they do not need the extensive catalog which they normally prepare; that a viewbook listing important aspects of the institution, major courses, and programs of study with a lot of pictures is all that is needed for recruitment; and that a descriptive list of courses can be published on newsprint and inserted in the viewbook for any persons wanting further information about courses taught. This kind of publication is likewise useful for high school counselors, junior college transfer prospects, and enrolled students who rely on expensive catalogs for a review of courses offered. Publishing on newsprint by offset means greater flexibility and the possibility of more frequent publication for considerably less money than the traditional catalog expenditure.

Beyond catalog costs, all colleges prepared brochures, viewbooks, and other mailings for prospective students. Institutions expended an average of $7838 for all publications, including catalogs, ranging in expenditure from $580 to $21,000. The average college in the study spent approximately $1500 for all publications other than the catalog used directly for recruitment and admissions purposes. This is quite a low cost per contact, averaging about 75 cents per person, excluding mailing and personnel costs required to get the material from the college to the prospect. Perhaps a more desirable expenditure ratio in publications would be to spend one dollar on materials designed expressly for parents and students and cut catalogs costs in half, thereby expending no more per prospect but aiming materials more specifically to the particular interests or needs of the market from which the college recruits.

Staff. The average college in this analysis employed 2.7 full-time-equivalent professional recruitment and admissions staff members. Staff range from one fourth of one person to 4.5 full-time-equivalent persons. The smaller the institution, the fewer the number of persons employed, although some of the smallest colleges employed as many as four people. This study was not able to determine any optimum size for the recruitment staff but did ascertain that for every full-time-equivalent staff member one hundred new students were enrolled in the institution in 1970–71. Again, this ratio is not meant to be a goal for the small college but simply a statement of present behavior. Experienced staff members should be able to recruit more than this number of students, and beginning staff members with effective training can be taught to reach this level more rapidly than the two years it traditionally takes to learn the job and become familiar with high school and church personnel and recruitment procedures.

There is little doubt that most of the nonselective private institutions in the present study employ too few people to accomplish the massive task assigned them in a time of declining enrollments. There is, on the other hand, no evidence that increasing the staff appreciably increases the number of new students. A longitudinal study could project the rate of enrollees in relationship to the rate of increase of staff and reach an optimum staff-size estimate. High-cost colleges in this project had larger recruiting staffs than the lower-cost colleges, paralleling the findings of the Carnegie Commission (1972 b, p. 146) and suggesting that the cost of recruiting students is directly passed on to the students enrolled. Dollars spent contacting and pursuing students who never come are secured from the students who do enroll.

The average annual salary of admissions directors in these institutions was $11,218 and in no way seemed to be related to institutional size, the smallest college paying as much as some of the largest. In terms of the average salaries paid to faculty, the admissions director receives an unreasonable income. Faculty (whose salaries are for nine or ten months) and the admissions director (who is usually on a twelve-month salary) average approximately the same pay. That is, admissions directors on the average receive approximately the same salary as assistant or associate professors in the college. But since admissions directors are asked to supply between 40 and 90 percent of all operating income for the institution, surely their salaries should be commensurate with their tasks. In no case did it appear that any admissions director was overpaid. Perhaps there is a direct relationship between the amount of money small colleges are willing to pay admissions directors and the number of students they are able to enroll. There is reason to believe that admissions directors and development officers ought to be receiving salaries equivalent to the president's when one considers the kind of responsibility they are expected to bear for institutional survival. Until colleges do pay more, they should not expect to get the results that they seek.

Most chief recruitment and admissions officers report to the academic dean. Forty-two percent are responsible to the dean, and 40 percent are responsible to the president. The remainder report either to the dean of students or the vice-president for development. The locus of responsibility for the recruitment and admissions program seems to be a matter of administrative expediency rather than institutional philosophy. If colleges perceive recruitment and admissions primarily as the first educational program of the institution, then it would be appropriate for those persons to report to the academic dean. If colleges understand recruitment as a student activity, then the dean of students is the appropriate manager. Or if they see recruitment as a primary function of institutional development, then the vice-president for development or the president might be the appropriate supervisor.

No matter who the direct supervisor may be, it is important that the director of admissions have access to all the administrative staff, especially the president. Dennis Johnson, one of the outstanding leaders of recruitment and admission practices in private colleges, supports this concept: "In order to emphasize both practically and symbolically the importance and centrality of the admissions process, the chief admissions officer should have a direct line to the president" (1971, pp. 169–170).

A direct line to the president does not necessarily mean that the president serves as supervisor, but simply that the admissions officer is able to talk easily and freely with the chief administrative officer of the institution and to know that the president understands the recruitment program, endorses it, supports it with his own efforts, and communicates that support both internally and to the constituents of the college. When this kind of presidential relationship exists, the direct supervisor of the admissions officer is not nearly so important. If, however,the supervisor is an academic dean, a dean of students, or a vice-president for development who tends to block access to the president or serves as a buffer between the president and the admissions director, the director probably should be reporting directly to the president, particularly if his salary and title, which might be dean of admissions or vice-president for admissions, are commensurate with the responsibility he holds for institutional survival.

Income and expense. The total expenditure for recruitment and admissions in these fifty small colleges, excluding catalog publication costs, averaged $43,754 but ranged from $5675 to $83,187. When the total expenditure for the admissions office was divided by the number of students enrolled, the average cost to recruit and enroll a student totaled $169. Recruitment costs are not a factor of institutional size, nor are total admissions costs related to institutional size. Table 19 portrays these and other average costs for all institutions by size.

The expenditure per student is slightly offset by the income

Table 19.

ADMISSIONS OFFICE AVERAGES IN FIFTY COLLEGES—1970–71

Item	Under 500	500–1000	1000–1500	All Colleges
Average per-student recruitment cost	$ 151.00	$ 177.00	$ 160.00	$ 169.00
Average application fee income per student	11.09	11.92	7.59	11.30
Average cost per catalog	.68	.63	.80	.65
Average annual salary for admissions directors	$10,656.00	$11,488.00	$10,000.00	$11,218.00

from application fees, which averages approximately $11.30 per application. In relationship to the expenditure to recruit a student, these institutions charge very little and probably could raise the fee as much as five dollars per student without affecting the number of applications.

The critical question about recruitment cost per student is the way in which the amount changes over a three- to five-year period. If it continues to increase more than 5 to 8 percent each year, then the admissions effort may be decreasing its efficiency and may be decreasing in effectiveness as well. If the cost decreases each year, then the opposite may be true, indicating either more students enrolled or smaller expenditure in the admissions office, or both. The desirable outcome is, of course, to hold expenditures constant or decrease them slightly and to improve the number of students enrolled. Virtually every recruitment and admissions program in the country is open to that possibility. Very few studies have been conducted of the efficiency-effectiveness ratio of the recruitment and admissions office. Data presented here suggest that such a study is feasible and would produce some needed guidelines for college administrators and trustees to help them know whether or not they are getting a good return for their dollar.

Figures in this recruitment study tell institutions only something of the range of possibilities and the averages in current practice. Institutions that fall below these averages have a goal, but institutions that are above the average are without a critical ratio of efficiency to effectiveness to guide their operation. Johnson again has been quoted as saying that additional staff is not the solution to the recruitment problem of most small colleges. The problem tends to be one of management of resources and ability to generate, assess, and respond to a particular clientele.

These two brief surveys of administrative functions reveal something of the kinds of data that need to be collected in order to make judgments about administrative practice. Not only have qualitative questions been raised in this discussion but some judgments have been set forth based on normative behavior and opinions of persons fully acquainted with the practices of small colleges. Institutions interested in analyzing costs and work relationships can follow the procedures outlined in these two brief reports, expand them considerably (depending upon the kinds of questions for which they desire answers), and come up with an excellent longitudinal profile of institutional behavior and production. Then a college can measure itself against the behavior of other institutions and know considerably more about the extent to which an effective program is being developed for the least number of dollars.

Chapter V

✕✕✕✕✕✕

Efficiency and Effectiveness

N umerous calls for efficiency in the management of small, private, nonselective liberal arts colleges have recently appeared. (McGrath, 1972; Astin and Lee, 1972; Bowen and Douglass, 1972b; Jellema,

This chapter is coauthored with Robert E. Knott, Ph.D. candidate at the State University of New York at Buffalo, who conducted the main body of research and wrote part of the manuscript.

1972)'. Each author who seeks more efficient management also notes that such efficiency is necessary but not sufficient for survival. In addition to efficiency, these colleges must maintain or improve the effectiveness of their programs. Certainly other variables—for instance, the existence and amount of state and federal aid, the continuation of private donations and foundation support, the rate of expansion or decline of enrollments—are critical to survival as well. But advice directed to the individual small college emphasizes that each institution must become an efficiently managed college with an effective program.

The relationship between efficiency and effectiveness is the focus of this chapter. Almost without exception, those knowledgeable and concerned about the future of the small, private liberal arts college arrive at a position similar to that of McGrath (1972, p. 132) : "The inescapable conclusion is that colleges must look inward toward more economical use of the resources they have (although, to be sure, they must continue to seek aid from all conceivable patrons)." Colleges that operate at a low rate of expenditure per student, however, are not necessarily efficient because of their poverty. The critical unanswered question underlying advice on efficiency is "How are institutional effectiveness and efficiency related?" or, as many higher educationists have put it, "Does institutional effectiveness decrease as cost per student decreases?"

Little reliable evidence is available which documents the limits to the benefits of economizing. Bowen and Douglass (1972b)' suggest a curricular restructuring that maximizes the use of faculty time and minimizes the expenditure for instruction. Advice is plentiful on the benefits of adopting program budgeting, the necessity of clarifying institutional goals, and the value of institutional research. But very seldom is the advice accompanied by careful supportive studies. As Bowen (1972a, p. 192)' concludes, "There is a dire need for facts about the relationship between [efficiency] and true educational effectiveness."

By examining the concepts of efficiency and effectiveness and applying them to three pairs of colleges which have been studied intensively, we may be able to reach some conclusions that can guide colleges in the future. It is the purpose of this chapter not only to analyze the relationship of institutional efficiency to effectiveness but also to draw conclusions from that analysis about how these institutions can reduce costs while maintaining or improving effectiveness.

The concept of efficiency in education is not new. It became widely popular some six decades ago, when educators responded positively to the publication of Frederick Taylor's *The Principles of Scientific Management* (see Callahan, 1962, pp. 25, 28–33). This work reflected the Progressive Era's strong push for reform and its influence on the business community. Taylor related the practice of the principles of scientific management to the development of efficiency. A business, in Taylor's view, is more efficient when it achieves greater productivity at the same cost. Specifically, a business becomes more efficient (1) by completing time-motion studies; (2) by standardizing tools and methods, establishing daily management objectives, and hiring and developing foremen to oversee newly designed practices; (3) by creating a department of planning and development to develop further the science of the job. Efficiency, then, was identified as both an end and a process.

In 1913, Frank Spaulding added the reduction of expenditures to Taylor's original formulation of increased productivity. Efficiency is the reduction of expenditure with the same or higher production. Although Taylor and Spaulding may appear to have been saying the same thing, the distinction in emphasizing the reduction of expenditure rather than the increase of productivity introduced the question "How low can expenditures go and still maintain a quality product?" This led Spaulding to define the educational product in units of student recitations. As a result, the question of product quality became one of product quantity, and the goal of an educational institution which desired efficiency was to reduce the "unit cost" (see Callahan, 1962, p. 76).

The most widely read and influential work on educational efficiency was Franklin Bobbitt's *The Supervision of City Schools*. Bobbitt sought to join the qualitative and quantitative dimensions of education with the concept of efficiency. He introduced two principles of efficiency management: (1) "Definite qualitative and quantitative standards must be determined for the product. . . . (2) When the material that is acted upon by the labor processes passes through a number of progressive stages on its way from the raw material to the ultimate product, definite, qualitative and quantitative standards must be determined for the product at each stage" (quoted in Callahan, 1962, p. 81). Bobbitt's work had a great impact on education by generating the standardization of materials, the classification of students, and the development of instructional objectives, but his ideas still begged the question of the relationship of quality and quantity. He assumed that quality and quantity were independent of each other and could be achieved once standards were established. A school could produce the desired results in quality and still reduce the "unit cost" by establishing careful standards to be met at all levels.

This conception of efficiency is defined as the reduction of expenditure with the same or higher productivity by means of processes in which each grade (or class) has standarized goals of quality and quantity. However, such a formulation based on class standardization is unnecessarily restrictive for the purposes of higher education. The critical elements are expenditures (inputs) and productivity (outputs). Placing these elements in relation to one another implies a process, but the standardization at class levels of the process is not essential (although "standardization" maintains a strong influence on higher education in the classification of students). Efficiency, then, is measured as a ratio between two variables: input and output.

If output is not defined exclusively in terms of productivity, an ambiguity is introduced. Emerson (1913) defined efficiency as the achievement of selected goals. These goals need not be, and often are not in higher education, defined solely in terms of quantifiable outputs. An institution may have definite and clear aims and be capable of achieving them but not be concerned with the minimization of expenditure in doing so. Is it still efficient? If so, then efficiency loses definition.

A distinction therefore needs be drawn between efficiency (a measure of the ratio between inputs and outputs) and effectiveness (the achievement of selected goals). Such a distinction is not always made by organization theorists. Litterer (1963, p. 55), for example, in his well-received text on organizations, defines efficiency in broader terms: "Efficiency of effort in the fundamental sense . . . is efficiency relative to the securing of necessary personal contributions to the cooperative system. . . . The emphasis now is on the view that the efficiency of an organization is its capacity to offer effective inducements in sufficient quantity to maintain the equilibrium of the system. It is efficiency in this sense and not the efficiency of material productiveness which maintains the vitality of organizations." It is possible to grant the insightfulness of Litterer's observation without adopting his concept of efficiency.

If, however, Litterer's definition were to be adopted, a monumental undertaking would emerge. One must define and operationalize such concepts as institutional vitality and equilibrium. On the other hand, for purposes of this chapter material productivity is too narrow a definition in that it elimates nonmaterial outputs from consideration. Hence, another conceptualization must be formulated which avoids the limitations of both too much and too little breadth.

If the concept of efficiency is viewed as a ratio between input and output, then efficiency may be defined as maximum output for a given input or minimum input for a given output (see LeLong, 1971). But how is input defined? Bowen and Douglass (1972b, p. 3), when discussing institutional efficiency, identify inputs with expenditures (or costs): "Efficiency is measured as a ratio between two variables: cost and output."

The term *cost* is substituted for the broader term *input*. Objections may be raised that more than monies are put into higher education. The faculty put in varying levels of competence and effort; students put in varying levels of skill, background, and motivation; administrators bring varying levels of expertise to their tasks; facilities are not comparable from institution to institution. The list seems endless. But it is possible to include inputs of a qualitative nature in the concept of institutional effectiveness. This allows the term *cost,* or *expenditures,* to be reserved for inputs in the definition of efficiency. The advantages of defining the concepts of efficiency and effectiveness in this manner are to establish a readily available measure of input which is comparable across institutions and still to deal in a responsible manner with important non-quantifiable elements of educational inputs. In *no* sense should this conceptualization of inputs be read as assuming that finances are the only critical inputs to higher education.

Efficiency, then, is a relationship between costs and outputs;

namely, the maximum output for a given cost or the minimum cost for a given output. It is the "optimal use of resources" (Moon, 1972, p. 74). But what is optimal? At what point does reduction of costs affect the quality of the output? At what point does dollar input no longer relate to quality? Since most institutions have not carefully defined the outputs desired and have not developed reliable measures to assess these outputs, conclusions about the efficiency or inefficiency of such institutions are suspect. At present, no one can determine whether an institution is delivering maximum output for given cost; only judgments of more or less efficient can be made by comparing two or more colleges.

The most difficult and debatable term in the definition of efficiency is *output*. Bowen (1972a) has observed that the efficiency of colleges and universities should not be judged by their role in educating students. Efficiency should be judged in part by the broad contributions that colleges make to society. However, other authors (for instance, Bogard, 1972) find that efficiency can be determined only when the outputs of the institution are quantitatively stated in relation to measured inputs. Since "broad contributions to society" do not lend themselves to quantification, either the efficiency of an institution cannot be determined or a restricted definition of outputs must be utilized.

Institutions of higher education do make broad contributions viewed from the societal perspective. They serve the economy by providing jobs, they keep youth from flooding the job market, they provide homes for artists and scientists, they provide opportunity for the constructive use of leisure time. But these and other contributions, although important to the conceptualization of the role of higher education in society, are stressed here only to the extent that the outputs not be defined exclusive of these contributions. Such exclusion, if widely adopted in practice, might remove from attention the consequences of change in management practices of the broader contributions. Otherwise, a more limited definition of outputs would be possible.

At least three dimensions of educational institutions serve as the foci of definitions of effectiveness. Inputs, outputs, and the environment have been considered the essential elements. Some authors find that institutional effectiveness is determined by the selectivity of the institution and its capacity to attract high-ability faculty and administraors. Others feel that the institutional products —faculty publications, student test scores—are the critical elements for determining institutional effectiveness. Still others focus on the environment—its type and emphasis, the development of the student from entry to exit—as the element of central importance in determining effectiveness.

Those who argue that the effectiveness of an institution is determined by its selectivity usually refer to the ability of the institution to attract able students and faculty as a measure of its vitality. Better sudents are capable of better work and, in turn, demand better performance from the faculty. The faculty expect more from these students and themselves, and the association of highly competent faculty with more able students creates a dynamic and productive environment.

A major limitation of the selectivity concept of effectiveness is that under this definition, no community or relatively open-door college—no matter how well it functioned to meet the needs of its students—could ever be termed an effective institution. Jeffersonian assumptions about the "weeding-out" functions of higher education underlie the selective argument: Since college *should be* for the exceptionally capable (in intellectual skills), only those institutions serving such students are quality institutions. Although prestige institutions do offer social contacts and many advantages to their students, it is unnecessarily restrictive to limit a conception of institutional effectiveness to measures of selectivity. Selectivity may be a measure of institutional reputation and visibility, but it may be unrelated to the rate or amount of learning or change occurring in students.

Another basis for determining institutional effectiveness is the degree to which institutions achieve their goals. Ikenberry (1962) has defined institutional effectiveness as the measure of the successful realization of institutional and instructional objectives; and such a definition does not necessarily involve the attainment of an arbitrary level of achievement. Certainly an institution can be effective without being efficient. It can do the right things without doing things right. (see Drucker, 1967, p. 71). But the achievement of goals taken by itself focuses no attention on the variation in expectations of achievement among institutions. Even the goals of highly selective institutions can reflect differing levels of expectations of their students.

The concept of effectiveness should include measures of input in relation to institutional goals as well as measures of output relative to input. This would permit intrainstitutional as well as interinstitutional studies. The concept of effectiveness is not so narrow as to be related only to individual institutions and their capability of meeting their goals, but neither is this factor to be eliminated from consideration.

Stuit (1961, p. 75) argues that the effectiveness of an institution "should be determined by measuring its products—what the institution does by way of developing the talents and attributes of its students and what it does to encourage productivity of its faculty." In fact, among the most often mentioned indicators of institutional effectiveness are student scores on the GRE, or similar standardized tests, and faculty publications. This argument again ignores what is done with students while they are at the institution; that is, it fails to account for levels of input and the goals of the institution. A student who enters college with a 1500 SAT score has an enormous advantage over one with a 600 SAT score when these students are competing to gain a high score on the GRE. Likewise, a faculty member who engages in six hours of instruction per week at an institution emphasizing research has advantages over a faculty member with fifteen instructional hours per week at an institution emphasizing teaching. Therefore, assessment of institutional effectiveness should include some measures of the ratio of input to output for a given institution. How far an institution develops its students' abilities in a given period of time should be included in measures of institutional effectiveness.

A final consideration in developing the concept of institutional effectiveness is that of institutional morale as an element of the environment. How do the faculty, students, and administration react to the institution? Certainly morale is a factor in the facilitation of institutional goal achievement, but it does not follow that high morale is superior to low morale across all institutions. Institutional morale must be viewed in light of institutional goals.

In summary, the concept of institutional effectiveness is

defined relative to its levels of input and output, the ratio of the two, and the institution's ability to achieve its goals in fashioning desired outputs from given inputs. Institutional effectiveness is best conceived as a profile based on multiple measures, rather than quantifiable with respect to a single measure.

This definition of effectiveness makes the task of relating institutional efficiency to effectiveness more complex. Difficulties are multiplied when institutions lack agreement on definition of outputs and fail to define institutional goals clearly. Rather than seek to establish an acceptable and comprehensive definition of institutional output (which is probably impossible at present), it seems best to operationalize the concept of effectiveness defined earlier by establishing selected indices of effectiveness and by comparing the relationship of those indices to measures of efficiency (costs) across institutions.

Methodology

This chapter builds upon the cost analysis presented in Chapters Two, Three, and Four, in which the sixty-six colleges were grouped by size of enrollment: under 500, 500–1000, and over 1000. From each group two colleges approximately similar in enrollment, but varing widely in the "cost per student" of their educational program, were selected. This categorization allows comparisons based on discrepancy of relative costs between colleges of similar size and among colleges of various sizes. Only the comparison-of-averages table was used to select the colleges. Names of schools were not known at the time. Any pair of colleges among the sixty-six could have been selected.

The popular wisdom of higher education says that the more money put into colleges and universities, the better the institutions. Increased income, with the resulting increased expenditure, generates higher faculty salaries, more library volumes, more Ph.D.s on the faculty, more instructional space, and lower student-faculty ratios. These, in turn, attract better students, produce more faculty publications and professionalism, and result in better-prepared and better-qualified faculty and students graduating from the institutions. If the popular wisdom that more money generates better programs is true, then these comparisons should show the higher-cost colleges with better programs.

Although there is reason to believe that the traditionally accepted indicators of quality educational programs are inadequate, this study will accept these indicators in order to determine whether or not they are related to cost. The purpose of the study is not to generate new indicators of program quality but to explore the role of educational expenditure in generating program effectiveness. The three pairs of colleges analyzed here should provide some insights into the relationship of educational costs and institutional effectiveness.

Each of the six selected colleges was studied intensively, using cost data already available and additional related data secured from the institution. Traditionally accepted input and output assessments of effectiveness were tabulated under four categories: faculty, students, general institutional, and alumni. Table 20 lists the items chosen as measures for faculty, students, and the institutions in general. Accrediting associations, both regional and professional, and the general literature of higher education served as the sources of items which historically have been used to accredit, approve, or commend the effectiveness of a college or university.

In addition to these standard items, an extensive alumni questionnaire was sent to all graduates of the colleges for the years 1961, 1966, and 1970. Data from alumni over a nine-year period included recent graduates and those who had been away from the campus long enough to make some seasoned judgments about their college experience. The alumni questionnaire included sixty-six items; thirty-two items were selected for tabulation because they were either "yes-no" or scaled responses. The scale of the responses was a continuum from 1 to 45. (See note for Table 21.)

The questionnaire was divided into three sections. Section 1 dealt with perceptions of the extent to which the college prepared graduates for professional, social, and personal roles. Section 2 dealt with graduate or professional study. All alumni who had attended graduate or professional school were asked about the effectiveness of instruction at their alma mater to prepare them for graduate or professional study. Alumni were also asked to compare their graduate and undergraduate educational experiences and to note those

Table 20.

INSTITUTIONAL STATISTICS—1970-71

COLLEGES

Item	Under 500			500–1000			Over 1000		
	Alpha	Beta	Difference	Gamma	Delta	Difference	Epsilon	Zeta	Difference
FTE students	469	473	(4)	687	692	(5)	1428	1180	(–248)
FTE faculty	44.48	33.28	(–11.2)	43.16	41.83	(–1.33)	89.58	83.03	(–6.55)
Cost per student	$1447	$2118	($671)	$1658	$2469	($811)	$1637	$1979	($342)
FACULTY									
Average salary	$8842	$9718	($876)	$10,115	$10,760	($645)	$9011	$7369	(–$1642)
Percent with doctorate	18.9	6.25	(–12.65)	23.8	72.5	(48.7)	30.6	30.8	(0.2)
Average credit-hour load	11.8	9.9	(–1.9)	9.6	12.0	(2.4)	11.9	13.0	(1.1)
Average class size	13.3	23.4	(11.1)	20.3	21.7	(1.4)	20.9	17.5	(–3.4)
Student-faculty ratio	10.5	14.2	(3.7)	15.9	16.5	(0.6)	15.9	14.2	(–1.7)
Average credit hours produced	309	437	(128)	558.5	735.9	(177.4)	476.6	439.9	(–36.7)
Average no. publications	0.51	0.22	(–0.29)	0.4	1.98	(1.58)	2.3	.61	(–1.69)
Average no. research projects	0.05	0	(–.05)	0.33	0.4	(0.07)	0.98	0.35	(–0.63)
Average no. professional meetings									
Attended	4.14	6.1	(1.96)	6.8	4.25	(–2.65)	11.5	2.5	(–9.0)
Addressed	0.08	0.44	(0.36)	0.67	1.85	(1.18)	1.25	0.94	(–0.31)
STUDENTS									
Average freshman SAT Scores									
Verbal	475	946.2ª	(5.2)	484	512	(28)	423.8	482	(58.2)
Math	466			508	534	(26)	451.2	475	(23.8)

Rank in high school class									
Top quarter	50.4%	38.9%	(−11.5%)	51%	44%	(−7%)	40%	50%	(10%)
Top half	83.2%	63.6%	(−9.6%)	81%	75.1%	(−5.9%)	72%	76%	(4%)
Average UGRE Scores									
Nat. Sci.	No	No	—	505	497	(−8)	No	No	—
Humanities	Data	Data	—	477	504	(27)	Data	Data	—
Soc. Sci.	—	—	—	436	446	(10)	—	—	—
Average GRE scores									
Verbal	519	No	—	424	No	—	No	475	—
Math.	489	Data	—	435	Data	—	Data	500	—
Percent graduates attending graduate or professional school	26.4	11.6	(−14.8)	25.2	52.6	(27.4)	18.8	18.2	(−0.6)
GENERAL									
Average sq. ft. instructional space	134.5	76.1	(−58.4)	105.8	68.4	(−37.4)	71.2	32.1	(−39.1)
Retention rate	64.4%	46.1%	(−18.3%)	44.6%	46.0%	(1.4%)	41.8%	44.2%	(0.4%)
Library									
Total no. volumes	52,329	40,500	(−11,829)	60,572	90,000	(29,428)	95,740	90,266	(−5,474)
Average no. volumes used	32.0	No	—	28.4	95.5	(67.1)	71.2	32.1	(−39.1)
Average sq. ft. library space	46.2	21.3	(−25.9)	24.1	19.0	(−5.1)	11.3	12.3	(1)
Institutional finances for faculty development	$4125	$6500	($2375)	$1999	$1000	(−$999)	$34,020	$9831	(−$24,189)
Administrative overhead on faculty salaries	1.1	2.4	(1.3)	1.4	2.6	(1.2)	1.7	2.5	(0.8)

a Converted ACT Sum score.

Table 21.

ALUMNI QUESTIONNAIRE SENT TO GRADUATES
OF 1961, 1966, 1970*

RESPONSE ITEM COMPARISONS

Colleges	Number Favoring High-Cost College	Number Favoring Neither College	Number Favoring Low-Cost College
Over 1000	4	17	11
500–1000	3	25	4
Under 500	13	16	3
	20	58	18

* All "yes-no" responses were entered into the analysis as percent of respondents answering "yes." The scale scores were weighted and averaged for the three years, and then a comparison of averages was made between the colleges for each item. The difference between the averaged responses was standardized as a percent of the total possible variation (4). Where the average scores on any item differed by more than 5 percent, the difference was considered important and entered as favorable to one or the other college. All average scores differing by less than 5 percent were considered as favoring neither college.

areas in which their undergraduate experience was particularly strong or weak. The third section of the alumni questionnaire dealt with employment. Questions were asked about the relationship of present employment to undergraduate education and about the effectiveness of their undergraduate education to meet the demands of employment. Finally, data on both beginning and present salary levels were requested.

The final source of basic information about institutional effectiveness came from the Institutional Functioning Inventory developed by the Educational Testing Service. The inventory records the perceptions of faculty, administration, and students about the environment of the college. The responses of these three campus groups are scored along eleven scale dimensions (six for students): (1)*intellectual-aesthetic extracurriculum*—availability of activities and opportunities for intellectual and aesthetic stimulation outside the classroom; (2) *freedom*—academic and personal freedom for all individuals in the campus community; (3) *human diversity*—the degree to which faculty and student body are heterogeneous in their backgrounds and present attitudes; (4) *concern for improvement of society*—the desire of people at the institution to apply their knowledge and skills in solving social problems and prompting social change; (5) *concern for undergraduate learning*—the degree to which the college emphasizes undergraduate teaching and learning; (6) *democratic governance*—the extent to which individuals in the campus community who are directly affected by a decision have the opportunity to participate in making the decision; (7) *meeting local needs*—institutional emphasis on providing educational and cultural opportunities for adults in the surrounding area as well as meeting the needs of local businesses and governmental agencies for trained manpower; (8) *self-study and planning*—the importance college leaders attach to continuous long-range planning for the total institution, and to institutional research needed in formulating and revising plans; (9) *concern for advancing knowledge*—the degree to which the institution emphasizes research and scholarship aimed at extending the scope of human knowledge; (10) *concern for innovation*—institutionalized commitment to experimentation with new ideas for educational practice; (11) *institutional esprit*—sense of shared purposes and high morale among faculty and administrators. No one pattern is ideal for all institutions using the IFI. However, the similarity of organization and purpose reflected in the six selected colleges permits easy comparison of scores, since parallel missions could be expected to generate like responses along the eleven scale dimensions of the inventory. The response scores are recorded in Table 22.

Each of the measures of effectiveness stands alone. No attempt was made to weight, scale, or relate them by category. On the basis of these evaluations, comparisons were made between the colleges in each pair to determine whether, in these schools, cost is related to effectiveness. Since the colleges compared had approximately the same enrollment and purpose, it should be possible to demonstrate or refute the relationship of cost per student to effectiveness.

Conclusions are drawn, where possible, about the relationship

Table 22.
Institutional Functioning Inventory Average Scores

Scale	STUDENTS						FACULTY						ADMINISTRATION					
	Alpha	Beta	Gamma	Delta	Epsilon	Zeta	Alpha	Beta	Gamma	Delta	Epsilon	Zeta	Alpha	Beta	Gamma	Delta	Epsilon	Zeta
Intellectual aesthetic	7.42	5.22	4.88	7.3	7.02	6.09	7.2	4.9	4.0	6.5	7.6	5.3	7.2	4.6	5.7	8.2	7.6	5.6
Freedom	3.39	5.16	4.17	6.2	6.19	8.05	3.3	6.3	4.8	7.6	8.8	9.1	2.7	5.1	4.9	7.8	8.3	10.5
Human diversity	4.21	5.02	3.24	4.0	5.79	5.00	3.7	5.7	3.2	4.7	6.5	5.9	5.1	6.5	4.6	5.3	5.8	7.6
Improvement of society	5.52	4.92	5.38	5.1	5.94	6.95	3.8	6.1	4.4	4.8	5.2	7.0	3.1	5.0	5.5	4.6	5.3	6.8
Undergraduate learning	9.58	8.94	8.27	8.3	9.33	9.35	9.1	10.3	7.6	9.4	9.4	9.9	8.6	10.6	10.1	9.7	9.7	10.2
Democratic governance	5.88	5.16	5.18	5.6	5.71	8.78	6.2	7.4	4.2	9.1	6.0	9.9	5.6	6.7	5.6	9.3	7.0	9.5
Meeting local needs	—	—	—	—	—	—	8.5	9.8	6.2	5.2	6.0	10.1	9.3	9.5	6.4	5.1	6.5	10.4
Self-study and planning	—	—	—	—	—	—	7.8	8.9	8.0	8.4	8.2	7.2	7.7	6.8	8.0	7.7	7.0	7.0
Advancement of knowledge	—	—	—	—	—	—	3.9	3.1	1.7	2.9	3.0	2.1	3.8	2.4	2.3	2.8	2.9	1.6
Innovation	—	—	—	—	—	—	7.2	8.8	6.8	9.1	9.7	8.9	7.1	9.1	6.5	8.2	9.2	10.4
Institutional esprit	—	—	—	—	—	—	9.4	10.1	7.8	11.3	9.4	8.8	9.0	9.0	8.3	11.6	10.5	10.0

of cost to effectiveness evidenced in the six selected colleges. While caution must be exercised in applying the conclusions to selective institutions, it is quite possible that the findings will prove useful to all colleges and universities because of basic similarities in organization, curriculum, and management practices.

Case Studies

The three pairs of colleges are identified by Greek letters. In each set the lowest-cost college precedes the higher-cost institution. The analysis-of-effectiveness indicators follow the categories described in the preceding section and reflect an effort to favor the higher-cost colleges whenever possible, since this is the direction of the literature and common wisdom.

Alpha and Beta colleges. Two Catholic-church–related liberal arts colleges for women were chosen for the case study of colleges with fewer than 500 students. Both are located in the Midwest and have similar purposes and missions. The subject offerings, majors, and numbers of FTE faculty and students are similar at these colleges, but they differ by $671 in the cost per student of their educational programs.

The high-cost college (Beta) pays a higher average faculty salary than does the low-cost college (Alpha). Beta also puts more money into faculty development, and its faculty attended and addressed more professional meetings during 1970–71. However, the difference between Alpha and Beta in other faculty professional credentials does not reflect the cost variance. The low-cost college (Alpha) has a substantially larger percent of its faculty with an earned doctorate and has a faculty more active in publishing than does Beta. Higher costs do not provide a more excellent faculty in this pair of colleges.

When measures of the instructional program are examined, Alpha has a smaller average class size, but faculty members carry a heavier credit-hour teaching load. The student-faculty ratio at Alpha is smaller, and Alpha provides substantially more instructional space than does Beta. Again, the higher cost does not provide the accoutrements for more effective instruction at Beta.

No consistent data were available for establishing the cogni-

tive achievement of students at these colleges. Beta sent fewer than
12 percent of its graduates to graduate or professional school and
did not administer any summative measures of student overall
cognitive attainment prior to graduation. Alpha also did not attempt
to measure the overall achievement levels of its students but did
send over 26 percent of its graduates to graduate or professional
school.

At entrance, Beta students were not better prepared. In fact,
Alpha tended to attract more students from the top quarter of their
high school class than did Beta. When the student SAT and GRE
scores for Alpha are compared with those of colleges in the other
size categories, it appears that Alpha did a creditable job of advancing its students cognitively. There is no reason to expect that Beta
would have superior performance in this area even if the comparative data were available. Higher cost appears not to correlate with
measures of student ability.

A look at general institutional data reveals that Alpha is
substantially more effective than Beta. Alpha provides more library
volumes and space, operates with a lower administrative overhead,
and has a markedly higher retention rate than does Beta. As noted
earlier, Beta provides more finances for faculty development; yet
this is not reflected in more consistent faculty professional development.

A different perspective on college life at Alpha and Beta is
provided by alumni responses (Table 21). The alumni of Beta did
give their college a more favorable rating than did the alumni of
Alpha. Beta's alumni felt more strongly that their college experience
provided them with a broad understanding of the political and social
forces affecting their lives, instilled a strong moral and ethical set of
values and provided valuable association with faculty. Alpha's
alumni, on the other hand, felt more strongly that their college provided a stimulus to attend graduate and professional schools, a reflection of the higher percentage of Alpha graduates who attempted
postgraduate study.

Caution is needed, however, in the interpretation of these
data from alumni responses. There were more items in which a
comparison favored neither college than there were items favoring
either of the two. Also, Beta had the smallest percentage of alumni

responses (35 percent contrasted with 45–50 percent for the other colleges) of all colleges in the study. If alumni more favorable to the college would be expected to return questionnaires, then the log in returned questionnaires would skew the results in Beta's favor.

The alumni responses serve to underscore the sameness between Alpha and Beta. The few stronger alumni item responses favoring Beta could be interpreted as providing a balance to the earlier statistics, which tended to favor Alpha; but there is no concrete evidence—such as higher salaries, more alumni in graduate study, or greater satisfaction with Beta—that Beta actually has a better-quality program. The higher cost of Beta is definitely not reflected in alumni perception of a more effective educational program.

An examination of the Institutional Functioning Inventory scale score (Table 22) for Alpha and Beta provides the perspective of present campus participants. The faculty and administration scores do not differ substantially from the student scores at either institution, which probably indicates a relatively low rate of friction on both campuses. The higher scores for Alpha on the intellectual-aesthetic scale reflect previous findings. There appears to be more freedom and greater human diversity as perceived by all groups at Beta than exists at Alpha. However, this does not hold for democratic governance, where Alpha and Beta appear approximately the same. Both colleges show substantial interest in undergraduate learning and a relatively high level of institutional esprit.

The Institutional Functioning Inventory scores reflect the strengths and weaknesses of the colleges. They add supportive data but do not introduce evidence to alter the conclusions previously reached. In summary, the higher cost of Beta is not reflected in a more effective educational program than that provided by lower-cost Alpha. Strengths of one college are offset by different strengths at the other.

Gamma and Delta colleges. The two colleges selected from the 500–1000 enrollment category are Protestant-church–related, coeducational liberal arts institutions. Both are located in the Northeast and, like Alpha and Beta colleges, have similar subject offerings, major areas, and overall missions. The numbers of students at the colleges are almost identical, but Delta College is $812 higher in the cost per student of its educational program. Do the educational programs of the colleges reflect the variation in cost in that Delta has a more effective program than Gamma?

Institutional profiles derived from basic institutional statistics (Table 20) suggest that traditional measures of program effectiveness do slightly favor Delta. In comparison with Gamma, Delta pays a higher average faculty salary and has more library volumes and a greater percent of faculty with the earned docorate. Gamma, however, has more instructional and library space and a lower student-faculty ratio than Delta. The faculty of Delta are more productive than those of Gamma in student credit hours, publications, and professional meetings addressed, although they also teach a larger average class and more credit hours per semester.

Are these faculty strengths reflected in student achievement scores? Apparently not. Although Delta attracts a slightly better-qualified sudent at entry than does Gamma, UGRE scores are not substantially higher for Delta's students. In fact, Gamma students score higher than Delta students in cognitive achievement in natural science. Therefore, the effectiveness of Delta's educational program relative to Gamma's is not firmly established. Most traditional measures of institutional effectiveness favor Delta, but even though more of its students go to graduate school, Gamma's students still score almost as high as Delta's on cognitive achievement. Some doubts must be entertained about the relative importance of such a great higher cost per student for educational programs.

An examination of the alumni questionnaire data fails to support the superior effectiveness of Delta compared to Gamma. Responses on twenty-five of the thirty-two items were so similar that no important difference between colleges could be noted. A larger percentage of Delta alumni did attempt postbaccalaureate study— probably because Delta alumni felt more strongly than Gamma alumni that college had stimulated their interest in graduate or professional school and aroused their curiosity and academic interests. Gamma alumni, on the other hand, felt more strongly that their college experience was directly related first of all to employment after college and to providing a firm set of values.

If the monthly salary of alumni, both beginning and present, is used as a criterion of college effectiveness, Gamma succeeds over Delta. Graduates from both schools earned almost identical average salaries at graduation (one dollar per month difference), but present average salary levels of Gamma alumni exceed those of Delta alumni by $99 per month. This difference could possibly be explained by noting the larger percentage of graduates of Delta entering postgraduate school and therefore delaying their realized earnings.

But in sum the comparison of alumni attitudes reveals no significant differences between Gamma and Delta with respect to graduates. This conclusion gives weight to the doubts introduced earlier regarding the superior effectiveness of Delta's educational program.

When the Institutional Functioning Inventory data are consulted in an attempt to clarify the comparison between Gamma and Delta, little of substance emerges. Delta definitely is perceived by its own campus constituents as placing a stronger emphasis on intellectual development and is characterized by higher faculty and administration esprit than Gamma. But a strong cautionary flag is raised by the discrepancy between student and faculty-administration perceptions of emphasis on undergraduate learning and democratic governance at Delta. The disparity of these scores (from 43rd to 70th percentile on undergraduate learning; from 19th to 86th percentile on democratic governance) moves away from alumni perceptions. Gamma, while not showing as high scores on institutional esprit or intellectual-aesthetic, does not evidence the same disparity among student and faculty-administration perceptions of campus life.

The real differences in Gamma and Delta tend to reflect a different concept of educating students more than a difference in program effectiveness. Gamma's students are more vocationally oriented and achieve quite well in this sphere, while Delta's students are more service and intellectually oriented and achieve well in that framework. Delta is perceived as slightly more intellectual and Gamma as getting students into careers more effectively. Since both colleges are consistent in perception and behavior, since both do what they intend to do fairly well, and since Delta, the high-cost college, does not produce significantly stronger graduates than Gamma, it is difficult to credit the input dollars that Delta spends on faculty with producing a more effective program.

It seems advisable to conclude that although the higher-cost program of Delta apparently does generate somewhat more positive institutional effectiveness scores on several items, the overall superiority of Delta is not clearly established. Therefore, the pattern of difference in cost but sameness in program effectiveness found in Alpha and Beta continued in this comparison of Gamma and Delta.

Epsilon and Zeta colleges. A Catholic- and a Protestant-church–related college were selected for the 1000–1500 size case. One is located in the Southeast the other in the Midwest. Again, both colleges are similar in curricular offerings, major programs, and overall institutional purpose. The colleges vary in number of FTE students by 248 and in FTE faculty by 6.55. However, the larger college (Epsilon) has the less expensive educational program and the larger faculty. Although the variance between the cost per student at Epsilon and Zeta ($342) is smaller than in the other two pairs, the fact that the larger college is the less expensive makes the cost difference more significant.

The $342 variation in cost per student should not be minimized on yet another count. When it is multiplied by the enrollment of Zeta (1180), an operating budget difference of $403,560 is generated, which is 17 percent of the educational budget of Zeta.

The basic institutional statistics in this study clearly favor the low-cost college. Epsilon pays its faculty more, and its faculty produce more credit hours. Epsilon has a more professional faculty by all measures. Epsilon's faculty teach a smaller credit-hour load than Zeta's. The Zeta faculty do teach smaller classes, and the student-faculty ratio is smaller at Zeta than at Epsilon.

The ability of entering students at Zeta is slightly better than at Epsilon. Zeta also draws a larger percentage of its students from higher high school ranks than does Epsilon, but the difference is minimal. Since no cooperative data are available for assessment of student cognitive achievement at Epsilon or Zeta, no final conclusions can be drawn about their relative effectiveness in this area. The GRE scores available for Zeta do not indicate that the achievement of its students is superior to the achievement of students at the other colleges in this study. Therefore, there seems no reason to expect a marked difference between these colleges in their effectiveness to generate cognitive achievement on the part of their students. This conclusion is supported by the almost identical percentage of alumni attending graduate school.

The general institutional statistics again clearly favor Epsilon. It has more instructional space and more library volumes (slightly less per student but greater student usage of library) than Zeta and almost the same library space as Zeta. Epsilon also puts substantially more money into faculty development than does Zeta. The administrative overhead on faculty salary is markedly better at Epsilon than at Zeta, reflecting fewer supporting costs for each dollar of faculty salary. These measures suggests that the higher cost per student of Zeta does not generate a more effective educational program for Zeta and that Epsilon is the more effective institution.

The alumni responses support the foregoing conclusion. Only four of thirty-two compared items favored Zeta. Eleven compared items favored Epsilon, and seventeen responses were balanced evenly. More alumni of Epsilon than of Zeta believed that their college experience demonstrated the value of a college education and provided productive association with faculty and fellow students. Epsilon's alumni were more likely than Zeta's alumni to send their children to their alma mater and would be more inclined to attend their alma mater if they were starting college again. More of Zeta's alumni felt that their college related directly to employment than did Epsilon's.

A comparison of beginning and present monthly alumni salaries of the two colleges shows that while Zeta's alumni averaged $18 more per month than Epsilon's at the beginning, Epsilon's alumni make $140 more per month presently. A further analysis of patterns in the beginning salaries of graduates of both institutions reveals that Zeta's alumni made more in 1961, both were approximately equal in 1966, and Epsilon's alumni made more in 1970. The disparity in 1961 salaries could be a reflection of the retarded economic condition of the Southeast in the early 1960s. In general, the analysis of the alumni responses supports the conclusion drawn from basic institutional statistics: Epsilon is the more effective institution.

The Institutional Functioning Inventory scores of Epsilon and Zeta evidence no strong data to substantiate or to contradict the foregoing conclusion. Epsilon scores slightly higher on the intellectual-aesthetic and the institutional esprit scales. Zeta scores higher on the freedom and democratic governance scales. Zeta also scores substantially higher than Epsilon on the meeting local needs scale. These scores show that Epsilon places more emphasis on scholarship while Zeta seeks to relate to local business and government needs. But neither college is clearly evaluated more positively than the other on any critical scale.

The conclusion that low cost per student and greater institutional effectiveness are joined in Epsilon goes uncontested. This case study, more so than the others, raises serious doubts about the popular notion in higher education that the more money put into colleges and universities, the better the institutions.

Not only is it possible to draw conclusions about each pair of colleges but also about the set of six. Modest differences exist among the group of colleges in the quality of graduates produced; but the colleges vary greatly in what they think necessary to produce these graduates, who act and think much alike. Cost per student differs as much as $800, average faculty salaries as much as $1600, teaching load by as much as one course a semester, and average class size differs as much as 40 percent among the six schools. Graduates' scores and alumni behavior and attitudes are much closer together, suggesting that cost is unrelated to effectiveness among the pairs of colleges as well as between them.

The higher cost of the less efficient college in each pair needs restatement. Contrary to usual behavior, all three higher-cost colleges had the smaller faculty. Pairs of colleges could have been selected in which larger faculties would account for increased cost without increased quality, but in these pairs administrative costs and student services were universally the primary cost overrun. Beta, Delta, and Zeta spent from 80 cents to $1.30 more on administration for every dollar of faculty salary than did Alpha, Gamma, or Epsilon. The higher-cost colleges could argue that they were establishing a richer environment than their counterparts. They may have more counseling, a better library, and more administrative services; but these do not seem to make a meaningful difference in the feelings of alumni or the record of graduates.

Beta has a higher faculty salary (by $876 per person) than Alpha, and the faculty teach a much lighter load (9.9 credit hours); both of these items add considerably to cost and probably could be changed without affecting program effectiveness. Delta also pays more per faculty member (by $645), with the same higher-cost result. Zeta faculty teach many more different courses offered to a much smaller average class size. As a result, they teach more hours and produce fewer student credit hours (thirty-seven fewer per person). Thus, in Zeta too many offerings require too many faculty, which increases cost.

This chapter purports to establish that higher-cost colleges do not necessarily produce better-quality graduates. Measuring absolute effectiveness or efficiency is not possible unless some arbitrary judgments are made about the validity of the measures now used for effectiveness. Probably the efficient college in each pair could be more efficient without decreasing its current level of effectiveness. Certainly the less efficient in each pair could be so. Likewise, the effective college in each pair probably could be even more effective without increasing cost.

Saying that cost and quality do not always stand in a cause-effect relationship among institutions does not preclude cost and quality from being directly related in a single college. In any given school, effectiveness, by definition, is related to efficiency; it is the ratio between cost and output. This analysis cannot comment upon behavior in any one college except to suggest that two critical questions need desperately to be answered: "What is the point in cost below which a college cannot go without decreasing effectiveness?" and "What is the point in cost above which quality is no longer improved?" These questions are answerable here only to the extent that comparable colleges with the same output but different costs (lower cost in one) can be found. Comparison is useful for disproving the universality of conventional wisdom and for exposing institutions which may be more or less effective or efficient, but no absolute conclusions can be drawn about effectiveness or efficiency in a single college.

Nevertheless, it is no longer possible to make categorical statements that higher cost means greater effectiveness among private institutions of similar type and purpose. It is not so. A single college may spend more and increase effectiveness or spend less and hold or increase effectiveness. It can also spend more and not affect effectiveness at all. This entire study suggests that colleges are more likely to spend more and not add to effectiveness than they are to spend less and detract from effectiveness.

Chapter VI

❧❧❧❦❦❦

Uses of Cost Analysis

The test of any planning effort is the positive gain achieved. The sixty-six colleges in this cost-effectiveness study demonstrated great gains from their participation. The uses they found for institutional assessment and cost analysis and the changes they made provide guidelines for all colleges that might undertake similar studies.

The sixty-six institutions were surveyed in 1973, one year after they had received our analyses. In this follow-up survey, each

institution was asked to describe in behavioral and attitudinal terms
any changes that had resulted from the cost study. Sixty institutions
responded with usable information. Four indicated by letter that
they were experiencing difficulties of one kind or another with the
cost data: either a new administration was not familiar with the
data or errors in what was submitted invalidated the ways in which
the college wanted to use the information. Two institutions simply
did not regard the study either as significant or worth their time once
it was completed. The bulk of the institutions, however, seemed to
gain from their participation and made amazing changes in only one
year.

The survey was divided into three parts. Each institution was
asked to indicate (1) the specific groups using the cost analysis data,
(2) the processes of using the data within the institution, and (3)
actual changes brought about as a result of the institution's use of
the data.

Groups Using the Data

The most extensive use of the data (in 91 percent of the
responding institutions) was made in academic long-range planning.
The data helped the colleges assess weak or problem areas of
management and were useful as background information for consultants working with curriculum and management in the institution. Several colleges with long-range planning committees gave
their cost study to the committee, which in turn used the report as a
basis for educating the faculty and student body about planning
decisions in process and for discussion and projection of future plans.
Other institutions used the data as guidelines for implementing
teaching-load reduction; for changing the number of majors, departments, and faculty; and for other direct decisions to be phased in or
out over a three- to five-year period.

In 56 percent of the institutions academic cost data were
presented in one form or another to the board of trustees, and several
other institutions indicated that they would soon be making pre-
sentations to the board. Data were presented in a variety of ways,
including full discussion of selected tables with the full board. Other
institutions used selected tables in annual reports prepared by ad-

ministrators and board committee members, and some boards discussed only the cost-relationship formula devised by Harris (1962, p. 519).

By far the largest use of the study with trustees was made through committees of the boards. The executive committee, the academic policies committee, the finance committee, and the planning committee of a number of the boards used data appropriate to their area of concern as a basis for analysis and preparation of specific policies for immediate implementation or for long-range planning.

Forty-one percent of the participants used the tables in proposals to foundations or governmental agencies. One college indicated, "In several cases major grants have been validated by the statistics and related evidences of good management." (Some colleges which used the data in their proposals were not funded, indicating that management information, although helpful, is not a panacea.)

Corresponding directly to the use of the data with foundations and governmental agencies in proposals, 65 percent of the institutions used the tables in the preparation of report forms for their church body or for the state or federal government. Accrediting associations have been recipients of numerous tables, particularly those comparing the institution under study with other colleges in the accrediting region. Because agencies ask questions in many different ways, colleges found it difficult to use any one set of data to respond to all questionnaires. The tables used in this project are simplified and consequently have a wider use than some of the more sophisticated computer-based cost analysis systems.

Another highly significant use of the data was in making decisions regarding immediate concerns in the academic area. Seventy percent of the institutions reported that the data were helpful in academic decision making, and 60 percent said that their academic decisions are now based on much firmer information as a result of their participating in the cost analysis study. Several colleges revealed that information not previously available in an organized fashion helped them to make meaningful decisions much more quickly and easily than had ever been possible before. Other institutions suggested that the data, maintained annually, would become increasingly valuable as faculty and deans became more sophisticated in using institutional research information for decisionmaking. Others said that they were moving in the direction of more responsible decisions.

Only one institution presented the complete study to alumni, although a number of colleges included statements from the study in annual reports and alumni publications as a basis for explaining institutional changes. One institution used many of the data in a presentation to regional alumni meetings.

Closely paralleling the small utilization with alumni, only 19 percent of the institutions felt that the data were useful in cooperative or consortia arrangements. Where used, data confirmed earlier decisions to develop cooperative programs, provided a firmer base for further cooperative arrangements, and established a basis for reexamining interinstitutional arrangements. Several of the institutions observed that other colleges in their consortia saw the need for a data base which, when developed, would improve relationships among the colleges, enable them to move collectively on data arranged in the same order, and consequently make more informed cooperative decisions.

Students were recipients of cost information in 41 percent of the institutions. Colleges which shared data with students were quite cautious. Some used the data to explain tuition increases or cutbacks in majors or other programs which would directly affect currently enrolled students. Others explained to students something of the decisions that administrators and faculty were required to make in a tight economy. But in 59 percent of the institutions administrators saw no reason to share the data with students, saying that the study had only indirect bearing upon students needs, that the study would not be understood by students, or that students had not asked for the information.

The colleges were asked whether external groups, such as foundations, government agencies, or alumni, responded positively to the study if they used it with them. Fifty-four percent stated that they did respond positively, that groups were requesting valid statistics as evidence of good stewardship, that the factual data were difficult to refute and clearly showed areas of need which helped the institutions receive funding. The accrediting associations commented positively about the use of the data in self-studies and requests for accreditation. One Catholic college indicated that the data were "excellent tools for establishing a better working relationship with the religious community sponsoring the college." In general, all institutions agreed that the groups with which they used the data were pleased to have the information and gained stronger and more positive impressions of the college and its management as a result of the cost analysis presentation.

Developing Data

Seventy-two percent of the institutions responding to the survey collected cost data for academic years other than the one prepared for them. Most of these have collected data for the years since the initial study in 1970–71, but a few went back to get information on 1968–69 or 1969–70 in order to provide a better historic profile of changes in the institution.

In 50 percent of the institutions the academic dean was primarily responsible for collecting academic cost data, but in 31 percent of the institutions the institutional research office responded to this task. Unfortunately, since most of the colleges in this study do not maintain an institutional research staff position, the dean or an associate such as the registrar was responsible for data collection. Nineteen percent of the institutions reported that either the business officer or the vice-president for administrative affairs collected the data from the various offices in the college and assembled them for analysis.

Working the raw materials into tables again was done primarily by the academic dean or business manager, although in institutions with an institutional research office (31 percent), a person in that office arranged the raw material into readable tables. Interestingly, in 26 percent of the colleges the president himself took the time to develop the tables for analysis.

Interpretation of the data was undertaken primarily by the president and the academic dean, although the business manager participated frequently. Initial interpretation of data was the responsibility of the department or division chairman in only seven of the institutions. Twenty percent of the colleges did indicate that faculty administrative committees appointed for the purpose worked together to analyze and interpret cost data gathered by the institution on itself.

Eighty-nine percent of the institutions reported that the data collected for them and the data that they collected themselves were primarily useful in immediately identifying high-cost areas. All colleges claimed that persons responsible for analyzing and interpreting the data understood both the study completed for them and those that they prepared themselves.

Only 11 percent of the institutions engaged outside consultants to read or interpret the cost analyses. Although some colleges are surfeited with consultants from the Council for the Advancement of Small Colleges and numerous other agencies, consultants can be of great help with institutions that have a firm data base and clearly understand the nature of their problem. Determining the problem is the first step in which a consultant must engage; if that is already clearly established by the institution, then consulting help can be precise, to the point, and considerably less expensive.

Changes Resulting from Data

Forty-eight percent of the responding institutions decreased faculty size, 30 percent modified faculty salaries, 43 percent increased class size, 43 percent reduced the number of courses offered, 37 percent changed the number of majors, 22 percent increased the total enrollment, 41 percent modified tuition, and 52 percent eliminated courses that were listed in the catalog but not taught. A number of other institutions made similar changes but not as a result of the cost analysis study. Such changes were in process before the study was undertaken or occurred independently of it. Modifications in enrollment, for example, were much more a result of recruitment efforts than of analysis of the relationship of cost to institutional size. Two institutions developed joint trustee-faculty-student committees on institutional priorities to read and interpret institutional analyses and to assist in establishing priorities for decision making, which would in turn modify factors such as faculty size and salaries, class size, number and type of courses offered, tuition charges, and cost.

The most critical question in the survey dealt with the extent to which colleges had experienced a major reduction in cost per student as a direct result of the cost study. Twenty-eight percent of the institutions indicated that a reduction had occurred. Several others suggested that had enrollments not dropped they too would have realized a reduction. Thus, it might be equally appropriate to ask whether institutions remained constant in cost per student even though they had a reduction in income and number of students. Given the situation of the private liberal arts college in today's market, to hold costs constant in an inflationary period and a time of decreasing enrollment is an accomplishment in itself. Some other institutions indicated that major reduction in cost per student could not be accomplished in a single year; however, by phasing out parts of programs and eliminating some staff and faculty positions, they expected to effect major reductions in cost within the next year or two.

Two thirds of the institutions reported actual behavioral changes as a result of the cost study. These changes included, in addition to modifications in actual numbers of programs and persons, a new awareness of the need for change within the faculty and administration, a better understanding of the relationship between the institution and other colleges of the same type and purpose, a willingness on the part of faculty to plan more meaningfully and more often, and a more sober approach to evaluating departmental offerings, taking into account cost factors in curriculum effectiveness.

Faculty across the nation responded positively to cost analysis, even when it revealed programs of exceptional cost or inefficiency. One dean stated that he "shared the results of the study with the faculty, who reacted positively to the data even where it was obvious that they worked harder than many other faculties. Fortunately, our pay is a bit above the average, so they saw a direct relationship."

The many pages of detailed modifications in program and personnel can be summarized into several categories. In one institution, for example, seven out of seventeen majors were eliminated, and in a number of other schools discipline majors were consolidated into area or interdisciplinary majors. Average class size was increased in many schools, and departments were consolidated; separate departments of sociology and psychology, for example, became one department of behavioral science. Courses were eliminated from the catalog if they were not being offered. One college dropped 40 percent, another dropped 50 percent of the courses listed in the catalog. Other institutions reduced the number of courses they were offering, some by as few as two or three but others by as many as twenty-five or thirty.

A number of institutions phased out faculty positions, dropping from one to seven full-time-equivalent faculty over a two-year period. Others increased the proportion of part-time faculty in order to effect economies by not committing large dollar outlays until the students were on the campus (since part-time people do not get paid if their courses are cancelled for lack of sufficient enrollment). A few colleges simply did not add faculty which they had projected in their long-range plan and were able to stay with the same number.

In the financial area several colleges instituted new audit procedures to provide more information for cost accounting. Others instituted stronger financial controls, so that they had a better idea where the dollars were going. One college developed new guidelines for policy making, relating academic decisions to cost; and several institutions reported that the cost data were serving as a basis for budget preparation for the coming year.

Two or three schools were able to reduce their administrative staff—in one case by as many as four persons. A president observed, "Some full-time faculty have been given administrative duties and reduced to part-time teachers, thus avoiding replacing administrators who have retired and enabling us to retain our faculty."

In the planning areas many institutions have begun to use the cost analysis data as a base for establishing an institutional research office and for developing a model for long-range planning. Another president said, "We have agreed on a percentage of the educational and general expenditures to be allocated to each major area and have established a three-year plan to reach these agreed-upon percentages."

Two particularly noteworthy instances of change based upon an analysis of the curriculum and related cost were noted by academic deans. One said, "We were anticipating these results and had already set a specific number of things in motion for which the study supplied confirmation. Faculty were reduced by eight, administrative staff was reduced by four, and 50 percent of the low-enrollment courses were eliminated." Another dean stated, "So far, we have experienced a change in attitude, particularly on the part of the faculty. They are looking at dollar implications of the educational program much more realistically. In the long run, we'll have a better academic program at less cost with better salaries."

Altogether, the colleges dropped sixty-four persons as a result of cost analysis. If the average faculty salary were applied to these (a conservative figure, since some are higher-paying administrative positions), the annual real dollar saving to this group of colleges exceeds $650,000. If the salaries of the persons projected to be added but not hired are included, the colleges save over $1,000,000 a year. The cost study cost the colleges collectively almost $30,000, resulting in a very handsome return on their investment.

Suggested Strategies

There are a number of actions most colleges can take if they have developed data comparable to those in this study or if they have been a part of any cost analysis project. Each of these actions has been referred to earlier but is reviewed here in with some suggested strategies for a full utilization of data.

Colleges can examine the number of their offerings, looking toward reducing the number of different courses offered each year in departments where more than approximately forty hours are taught. Faculties can develop policy statements on course additions and deletions—policies, for instance, that require a department to eliminate one course for every course added. Sterling College in Kansas developed the checklist shown in Table 23 for every course in the department and asked departmental faculty to justify the courses they offered on these bases.

Colleges can easily eliminate courses listed in the catalog but not taught for two years. Administrative and faculty persons responsible for material in the catalog can determine a policy whereby courses are dropped. One solution utilized by some institutions is to

Table 23.
FACULTY EVALUATION OF COURSE—STERLING COLLEGE

Department ....

Course Name and Number ....

	Yes	No
1. Is this course required for the major?	....	....
2. Is it required as a supporting course for some other department?	....	....
3. Is it required for the Competency Curriculum? (Core)	....	....
4. Is it one of the alternatives listed under a Competency?	....	....
5. Has the course had an average enrollment of ten or more students, when offered, over the past five years? If the answer is no, please place the average enrollment figure in the box at the right.	....	....
6. If the course has been offered for fewer than ten students during the past five years, is it because it is required for a major?	....	....
7. Does the course serve as one of several alternatives for the major?	....	....
8. Could this course be eliminated?	....	....
9. Could the content of this course be combined with that of another course in this or another department?	....	....
10. Could the time used for this course be combined with the time used for another course to give a longer course (e.g., two three-hour courses combined to give one four-hour course)?	....	....
11. Could this course be offered during the summer or interterm rather than during the semester?	....	....
12. Could an equivalent course be obtained outside the institution (e.g., a consortium course)?	....	....
13. Could an equivalent course be obtained within this institution, but outside this department?	....	....
14. If there are other reasons which would justify the continued offering of this course, please give them in the space below.	....	....

eliminate all course listings from the catalog and publish instead an annual or a semiannual newsprint supplement to the catalog that lists the courses to be offered that particular term.

Faculty committees can examine the number of majors. Most liberal arts colleges have developed a large number of majors and, as times have changed, have added to that list without subtracting many, if any. Although group majors such as liberal arts, humanities, social sciences, and natural science are increasingly unpopular because they do not appear to lead to any vocational or professional career, there are a number of combined majors that can be meaningful without greatly increasing institutional expenses. Career-oriented majors are quite popular, and combinations of these in the social sciences would be particularly inexpensive. A college could develop new majors in middle-management areas for city, county, and state government and for service agencies such as police and fire departments, welfare, and a variety of community agencies, including second- and third-level hospital administrators and staffs. The role of women in banking, commerce, and industry is increasing, with correspondent needs for expanded majors which aim their programs more directly to roles that women play in these fields today. In a number of small colleges there are expensive majors which could be eliminated without any loss of enrollment or prestige. Sterling College also has a checklist for justifying each major (see Table 24).

The financial reporting and auditing processes in many small colleges leave much to be desired. Administrators can use the data base as a test of financial reporting and auditing to see whether they are getting the information they need for decision making, cost accounting, and proposal development. If not, changes should be instituted as rapidly as possible.

Faculty productivity can be examined on the basis of these cost data. Since faculty productivity is comprised of teaching load and class size, perhaps small classes should be eliminated—unless they are necessary for majors or are part of a conscious program such as independent study and tutorials. Faculty can establish policies that courses of fewer than five or ten students will be eliminated and faculty loads redistributed among the necessary offerings. Both policies and a number of others increase class size without

Table 24.

EVALUATION OF MAJOR—STERLING COLLEGE

Major ....

1. How many majors graduated each year for the past three years?
   1970 .... 1971 .... 1972 ....

2. What proportion of graduates with this major get jobs or go to graduate school in an area related to the major?
   1970 .... 1971 .... 1972 ....

3. Is the number of students interested in this field at this institution increasing or decreasing?

4. How many students majoring in this area could be handled with the
   present staff?

5. List the career areas open to graduates with this major.

6. Does this major contribute to the cultural enrichment of the institution
   and/or the community? How?

7. Does this major contribute a service to the institution and/or the community? How?

8. Is this major critical to the continuation of this college? Why?

9. Could this major be combined with another major to form a new one?
   How?

10. Does this major enrich the general education program of a liberal arts
    college? If yes, how?

11. Could this major be eliminated? If yes, in how many years?

adding hours to the teaching load. As a result, faculty productivity
is increased and institutional cost decreased without affecting the
quality of the program in any way yet determined.

Cost data can be used in program budgeting and cost accounting. Program budgeting can be defined simply or elaborately.
In this instance it can mean only that each program unit of the
institution develops a budget based on programs rather than upon

traditional items. Each program budget is comprised of several items such as staff, equipment, supplies, and supporting help. Then the program area budget is developed on priorities, with the most critical programs listed first and the least important programs last. The budget committee—instead of cutting or adding a straight percentage to each area or, even less appropriate, instead of putting money where the most noise occurs—can allocate institutional resources in terms of priorities established in each budget area. This means that whole programs are eliminated and others maintained at a sufficient level to operate them effectively rather than reducing the effectiveness of each program within the institutions. Likewise, simple cost accounting (as detailed in Chapter Seven) can be instituted on the basis of these data. From this base a much more elaborate scheme of cost accounting can be developed—a scheme that takes into account all the indirect costs and establishes formulas for plant facility utilization, percentage allocations of library cost, student services, and a large number of other supportive activities which are not included in this study.

As Chapter Seven shows, curriculum and cost data can become the basis of long-range planning and the development of an office of institutional research. Very little more needs to be said about this possibility, since this is the central use for a data base and certainly the most easily understood use by all constituent groups of colleges and universities.

The data can be used effectively by administrators to explain institutional behavior and decision making to trustees, faculty, students, and alumni. Each of these groups needs to have different information, couched in language with which they are familiar, phrased in such a way that the technical aspects are removed. It is, of course, possible to provide people with too much information or not enough information, so that they are overwhelmed or left wondering if the presentation is trying to hide some factors which would not put the institution in the best light. Trustees most appropriately need to know something about the base of management and are helped to understand the predicament of the small college by comparing one institution with others of the same size and purpose.

Externally these data constitute a very excellent base for proposals to foundations, corporations, and government agencies.

Persons who give away money are increasingly concerned about institutional management. They look carefully to see whether their funds will be well managed and will produce the desired results proposed by the college seeking dollars. To lay out in a proposal the exact accounting policies, procedures, and conclusions with comparative data cannot help but enhance the chances of an institution's being funded. Government reports, although not all alike, can be more easily answered if the college has a good data base that can easily produce as many different categories of answers as possible. Accrediting associations, likewise, are particularly pleased to receive comparative data about institutional management; such data enhance the ability of these associations to make a judgment about the way in which a college asking for accreditation or in the process of reaccreditation has managed its institutional resources, both human and physical.

Some institutions have, of course, found additional uses for the data and have expanded on the suggestions made here. These are the primary ways in which colleges have used the data and can use them effectively. The list is sufficiently long and the record of change sufficiently strong to warrant the conclusions that all colleges should develop a program of academic and administrative analysis with cost applications.

Case Statements

The following cases illustrate in detail ways in which three small colleges have improved their management and financial position as a result of using these cost studies in long-range planning, institutional research, and day-to-day academic decision making. Extensive conversations with academic deans in these institutions produced the brief descriptions that follow. The most important aspect of the case statements is not the excellent changes which the institutions have achieved but the strategies by which they proceeded while at the same time maintaining high faculty and student morale. The most damaging aspect of institutional cutback is, of course, the of confidence that students, faculty, and in turn alumni and prospective students experience if they think a college is on the decline. These cases document the possibility that institutional changes can be made which produce greater efficiency and effectiveness without loss of morale or forward motion.

The three institutions have used the cost analysis in various ways in developing institutional plans. College X used the cost data primarily for making day-to-day decisions more effectively and in short-range planning. College Y utilized the data in a long-range planning process which was undertaken without data but revitalized, reshaped, and improved after the introduction of the cost data. College Z used the data base as the impetus for developing an extensive, comprehensive planning program. Each college represents a different way of using institutional data with a different depth of understanding by administrators, faculty, students, trustees, and alumni.

College X. On the basis of the academic cost analysis survey, College X developed a data-interpretation mechanism and changed strategies for institutional decision making. Without developing a long-range plan, the staff laid the groundwork for planning when the faculty is ready to move into it. Administrators interpreted institutional data to a variety of constituent groups for a full year before proposing action on the interpretations.

At the onset the president, using tables prepared from the comprehensive study by the business office, presented selected data in his annual report to the student body and faculty in an assembly. He summarized the 1970–71 year and handed out printed copies of the annual report. In addition, he presented data to the executive policies committee of the board of trustees, and the academic dean presented the full data to the faculty in divisional meetings. The divisional chairmen and the executive policies committee of the board were both concerned with academic affairs and consequently reviewed all the tables describing the academic program. Students in College X serve on faculty committees and have representatives on the division chairmen's committee, which also serves as the dean's advisory council; students thus were privy to data discussion and analysis, not only in summary in an assembly but by way of membership on all committees of the faculty.

The dean interpreted data first to the division chairmen and then to all faculty, going personally to monthly divisional meetings. The dean's presentation focused on the concept that "quality programs can still be maintained even though we use cost as an instrument of change." The dean reported that the faculty were initially apprehensive but, because they could pose no alternatives to the facts presented, accepted the data as a basis for needed changes. The dean presented data sheets, tables designed specifically for each division, outlining all pertinent information related to that administrative unit. In his presentation he used transparencies on an overhead projector and then left the data sheets with the division chairmen for discussion within the division.

Prior to the cost analysis of 1970–71, the dean and members of his staff had conducted some studies that revealed the same trends; but, because they were not specific or detailed, the studies were not acceptable to the faculty. The comprehensive nature of the cost study finally convinced the faculty of the validity of the enterprise.

The primary strategy developed by the administration of the college was to organize a joint trustee-faculty-student "committee on priorities" to assist in day-to-day decision making and in determining the priorities of the budget. Division chairmen were not allowed on this committee but instead were asked to choose six key faculty members. The students chose student representatives, and the trustees chose their representatives. This committee was extremely influential within the faculty and trustee board in helping the dean and the president determine institutional priorities in terms of budget making and funding sources. In the judgment of the president, this committee was essential in helping to bring about changes that resulted in a tighter financial program and a balanced budget. The committee was disbanded after it had served its purpose, but there is strong agitation within the faculty in College X to restore it as a permanent "watchdog."

Several actions were taken as a result of data dissemination and the development of the priorities committee. A tenured faculty member was dropped in chemistry, after having been notified a year in advance that such a proposition was under study, that the chemistry program was entirely too costly, and that the cost analysis data pointed directly to the need for a change in this area. As a by-product of this action, the tenure provision in the faculty manual was updated and the institution adhered more closely to AAC and AAUP policy recommendations for tenured faculty. Part-time faculty were hired to handle needed service courses in music and in chemistry, but the major and the primary program were disbanded.

Such an action, of course, brought about a number of institutional problems but produced some positive responses as well. Full-time faculty did not like the move and responded adversely. The dean admitted that hiring part-time faculty—people who "were not tied into the mainstream of institutional life"—was not pleasing to the full-time faculty. On the other hand, the dean was able to convince the full-time faculty that such a move actually strengthened and enriched the core of remaining faculty. Specifically, part-time people could supplement the competencies of the full-time faculty; in addition, the full-time people could concentrate on some of the activities ancillary to teaching, such as advising and managing the institution's programs.

Beyond changes within the faculty and the addition of part-time personnel, stronger budget controls were instituted in the business office. Cost data and institutional research data have been gathered each year since 1970–71 and put on the computer to which the institution has access. Now all administrators and division chairmen receive monthly reports detailing cost and all other variables paralleling tables prepared in the 1970–71 cost analysis. A data base, updated monthly, undergirds all faculty, student, and administrative day-to-day decision making.

College Y. College Y followed a different path. In 1969 the college planned a complete revamping of curriculum, to become effective in 1971. The interim period, 1970–71, was to be a time of assessment of institutional priorities and directions for the future. During this time communications between students and faculty, faculty and administrators, administrators and trustees were refined. In the middle of the 1970–71 year the cost analysis data were completed for the 1969–70 academic year. Data were compiled and analyzed for subsequent years as well; but on the basis of the initial assessment, which occurred during the evaluation year 1970–71, all groups within the institution reviewed and began to act upon the data. The board of trustees reviewed the data with the faculty through the help of a consultant, who made an initial presentation and helped the college community interpret the meaning of the data.

Regular developmental dinners were held to bring trustees

and faculty together as "peers and colleagues" and as a means of breaking down adversary viewpoints. This strategy was very helpful in informally explaining and later implementing needed changes from both sides. It helped to cultivate good will and was especially important in a young college with a relatively young faculty. The development officer has been the primary person responsible for developing internal institutional cooperation. She is committed to institutional self-renewal and serves as the primary change agent in the institution.

As a result of the cost analysis study in an institution already geared for long-range planning, a number of activities occurred. For instance, the mathematics major was phased out, and students were invited to continue mathematics through cooperation with a nearby institution that offers such a major. The strategy for developing this concept began when the mathematics department chairman from the cooperating institution was hired as a part-time lecturer; this chairman, in turn, helped to establish a productive relationship with his own institution so that students could take mathematics courses there. Based on that success, College Y is seeking cooperative arrangements with other colleges in the area that have, for example, more extensive and more expensive laboratory facilities. Eventually College Y hopes to offer a broad variety of majors on campuses of adjacent institutions.

The faculty has been quite receptive to all the changes made in the institution, primarily because of the presentation of the data and the attitude of careful planning with implementation postponed until full thought could be given to all aspects of change. Through increases in enrollment, student-faculty ratios have been raised from 1–11 to 1–17 with no negative feedback from the faculty. Teaching contact hours have been examined, especially in sciences, nursing, and medical technology—all fields in which the teaching hours were quite low. Laboratories are given some contact-hour credit in a unit ratio devised jointly by the faculty tenure committee and administration.

Budgeting procedures are much clearer and firmer as a result of the cost study. College Y always has had reasonably good budgeting procedures but has had difficulty in interpreting budget income and expenditure reports to faculty, administrators, and trustees. Now the faculty are actively involved in budgeting at the departmental level, as are all administrative units; and each in turn is an effective channel of necessary information about cost effectiveness.

The institution has revitalized itself as a result of the cost analysis. Resources immediately available were tapped for the first time. The enrollment increased 41 percent almost entirely through developing programs for older women, which completely erased an institutional deficit of $38,000 in one year.

The faculty are considerably more aware of the need to maximize enrollment in electives and advanced courses. They made a careful study of students who will be attracted to elective courses, developed programs according to market assessments of older students potentially available to the institution, and correspondingly developed their courses to attract people from outside the institution rather than just teaching courses which faculty members wished to teach because they were a specialty or particularly attractive to them individually. As a result of cost studies and consequent long-range plans, the faculty developed three new majors by hiring only two new individuals. These changes reflected careful planning, sorting courses to be retained in the curriculum and dropping all those that were not enrolling sufficient numbers of people to be economical.

Because of the small size and intense socialization of this eastern women's college, change occurs quickly. But before they launched any institutional changes, the dynamic administrative staff carefully shared cost information with faculty and educated them in the ways in which these data should be read and understood. The changes that occurred came about as a result of combined effort of faculty, trustees, and administrators. They are likely to be long lasting because enrollment has increased and cuts have not been necessary, generating an increasingly higher institutional morale and desire to continue to change on the basis of sound evidence. Long-range planning is a pleasure at College Y for all concerned.

College Z. Continuous formal planning has been a three-year process at College Z. Beginning in 1970–71 College Z started a planning process under CASC sponsorship. As a result of the cost study, in 1972–73 the college assigned a staff member responsibility for institutional research and planning. With the doubling of enrollment in five years and considerable curriculum change, it became necessary to have a qualified person, full time, assessing the present condition and possible futures of the college. This person, the director of planning and program development, reports directly to the president.

The director calls the office "a radar station, receiving signals from the outside as well as from the inside, communicating these to our constituencies, encouraging faculty and staff to use the office as a change agent." Because of two previous years' experience, the present office undertakes planning, institutional research, and direction of a study committee on interinstitutional cooperation. The director of planning and program development chairs the planning committee. This committee has an overarching function in the college and reaches into all the segments of the institution. The college is engaged in continous planning and keeps a five-year projection active at all times.

Membership on the planning committee, which is chaired by the director of planning, includes the president, chief academic business and student affairs officers, the director of admissions, and representatives of the board of trustees, the faculty, and the student body. Each year the committee sets tasks for itself and appoints teams outside the committee but chaired by a committee member to undertake the research and prepare planning strategies or position papers. Each task force is also divided into smaller segments, called "study units," under the direction of a member of a task team. Altogether, in a college of a little over one thousand students, ninety-five people, one third of them students, were engaged actively in planning in 1973. The four task teams and their study units are as follows: Task Team I, the student development team, studies housing and development, student government, the "drop-in center," the health service, and security. Task Team II, on curriculum development, concentrates on such matters as grading, continuing education, health programs, faculty development, and independent study. Task Team III, concerned with management and development of financial resources, studies news information, fiscal resources and management, the arts center, and development in general. The fourth task team, on governance, studies administrative structure, academic committees, student government, the presidency, and the trustees.

The work of the task teams and the planning committee is summarized in a planning report. It is a rather extensive piece, bringing together the work accomplished as well as recommendations in the five-year projection in all of the areas of the study. The planning committee is also the budget committee at the college. A major period of time in December and January is spent working on the budget. Gradually, the budget process is becoming a total college concern, involving nearly one hundred persons directly.

The impact of the establishment of a major planning office is just beginning to be felt. The director annually updates the cost analysis as the primary data bank for the college and then conducts other studies to support planning. Increased involvement of faculty, students, trustees, and second-level administrators, with concomitant increased communication, has been the major value of this office. But the entire college community has an enhanced awareness of a need for clarity of mission, identity, and purpose and fully understands and supports the need for a solid data base, continuous evaluation, and continuous planning.

Colleges X, Y, and Z, operating at different levels, demonstrate what all colleges could be doing to develop themselves if they maintained a reliable, continuously updated cost analysis as a base and if they utilized some of the strategies outlined by colleges in this study. Saving a million dollars a year should be incentive enough, but the less tangible benefits—like knowing what you are doing and where you are going and that morale is high while you are getting there—may be even greater in the long run.

Chapter VII

❧❧❧❦❦❦

A Comprehensive
Planning Strategy

Not only is this book an account of values gained and strategies employed by one group of colleges that did change; it can also serve as a guide to other institutions that want to follow the same path to greater cost effectiveness. Self-sudy and planning are the obvious

The author is indebted to *Liberal Education* for permission to reprint in greatly revised form excerpts from his article in the October 1967 issue.

possible outcomes of careful cost analysis. This chapter details the terminology and procedures for developing a program of cost effectiveness incorporated within a comprehensive long-range plan.

Building a Data Base

Focus on planning must of necessity first center on sound records. One criterion for keeping records is to hold only those that are up to date or useful. Records that are useful for operating decisions, for reporting to central management, for planning and evaluation, and for decisions by administrators and trustees should be kept. If an institution followed these four criteria for record keeping, it could probably combine or throw out many records that have for years been stored in some attic or basement. Some colleges have gained whole new classrooms by revising their record-keeping criteria.

Very few records are necessary for cost analysis and planning. Forms necessary for collection of data on students, faculty, curriculum, and finance (Forms 1 through 6) appear at the end of this chapter. These data are essentially the information necessary for all the cost studies, curricular analyses, and administrative analyses outlined in this volume. Thus, a very small data base can produce a great amount of information about the institution without the necessity of a computer or a full-time institutional research staff. There are, of course, numerous computer-based data retrieval systems, ranging in design and price from very modest to hundreds of thousands of dollars. Some systems designed for small colleges work with eighty-four different variables and provide an institution with a printout as often as any of the eighty-four variables changes, with projections for two, three, five, or ten years. These elaborate systems can be helpful if institutional decision makers are sophisticated enough to utilize the wealth of data produced. Otherwise, a great data overload exists, and faculty committees and administrators are overwhelmed by the amount of information before them; as a result, decision making and planning are based on intuition and observation while the data lie on the table ignored.

There is no substitute for a comprehensive data base. Without it no planning can be carried forward, no institutional projections can be made, and no effective cost changes can be instituted. An institution can compile an adequate data base by using the aforementioned guidelines and by reviewing data collected in earlier chapters of this book (see especially, Chapters Two and Five). Colleges participating in this study discovered that they could collect the necessary data for a given semester within two working days; and, once systems were established for retrieving the information, it could be brought together in even less time. Institutions which then proceeded to analyze and interpret their own data after an initial evaluation was made for them discovered that the whole operation, including data collection, could be completed in ten days. This kind of effort should not tax any college and is more than worth the dollars, even if the effort must be contracted from the outside because no faculty members, senior students, or administrators feel they have time to undertake the task.

Data Analysis and Interpretation

The greatest impetus to the development of a comprehensive planning and cost accounting strategy is the establishment of an office of institutional research. Institutional research is an analysis and interpretation of data about a college—an interpretation based on some assumptions made about the society (the religious, economic, sociopolitical, and educational conditions) in which the college exists.

Institutional research differs from a self-study in that institutional research involves only trained researchers—or at least the psychologists, sociologists, and statisticians of the faculty—in basic data collection separate from any judgment about their meaning. This kind of analysis should not be related to decision making, but rather should consist of gathering the "stuff" on which decisions can be made in the future. Institutional research is not concerned with consensus or valuing but simply with reporting what has been, what now is, and, all things being equal, what will be the situation of a college. It always precedes a self-study and long-range planning, since it provides the material on which these can be based.

Institutional research focuses on data organization and dissemination and is limited to the components of an educational institution. Data on these components (curriculum, philosophy, structure, students, faculty, facilities, and finances), once analyzed, serve as a basis for comparative studies and as a benchmark for decisions. Additionally, qualitative types of data must be gathered—through the use of social science research techniques such as case studies, perceptual studies, and surveys, as well as purely descriptive statistical methodology. Finally, all data collected should be viewed in the dimensions of past, present, and future.

Data need to be kept current each year. It is not worthwhile to collect them only once. The first time is the hardest; after records are initially established, it is relatively easy to fill in the figures on the same tables each year. By keeping useful records of the past, a college can see trends over the last few years which make a great difference in helping to know where it can move in the future.

The Council for the Advancement of Small Colleges, in a project under the direction of William Shoemaker, has developed a pilot study and is in the process of preparing manuals which can help small colleges establish and train part-time or full-time faculty or administrators in data collection, analysis, and interpretation as well as developing more sophisticated studies in market analysis of prospective students, attrition and retention, and evaluation of all parts of the collegiate program and management.

Institutional research has several values for a college. Data provide a historical picture of change as well as the basis for questioning the desirability of change. An institution may very well not want to change, feeling that its present course is satisfactory. Also, data provide the basis for making predictions about the future, which gets into the area of valuing or goal setting.

Cost Analysis Strategy

One of the first major functions of an institutional research office is to make a cost analysis of the college's programs. Cost analysis is a general term used to describe a three-part concept composed of cost accounting, cost-effectiveness analysis, and cost benefit. Cost accounting is essentially the act of determining the cost of a single program or educational unit, taking all the costs related to a particular objective or program and grouping them together. Costs are measured not only in dollars but in resources, so that cost accounting includes grouping the resource requirements of a program together with their related dollar costs. Chapters Two and Five of this book are essentially statements of cost accounting; that is, groupings of resources and related dollar values in terms of a single or several common denominators such as faculty productivity, student credit hour, class size, and other factors of the educational program.

Cost-effectiveness analysis is a much more complex concept and is the heart of the cost analysis idea. It is the act of comparing the relationship between input and output, between the resources and their related dollar costs and the achievement of desired goals, competencies, or other outcomes. As a technique for comparison, cost-effectiveness analysis can (1) help assess the relative worth of several programs with the same educational outcome—for instance, a group of departments in the natural sciences all of which produce majors who are tested on the Undergraduate Record Examination in the sciences; (2) determine whether a single program is becoming more or less effective as time passes; (3) help assess the relative worth of the same program for different groups of people—for instance, the value of an admissions program with church constituents, students from minority groups, or alumni contacts; and (4) act as a useful device for comparing programs among institutions of similar purpose and types of programs. Chapters Two and Five suggest some cost-effectiveness analyses.

Cost-effectiveness analysis is a qualitative judgment made about the relationship of cost to outcomes. Questions are asked such as "Are the funds being used efficiently?" "Would the same results be achieved with a different program approach that might cost less?" "Would the same gain per student be achieved for less money?" "Could greater gain per student be achieved for the same money?" "Could greater gain per student be achieved for less money?" When these relationships are determined by pretesting and posttesting or other assessment mechanisms and the related costs are fully determined, alternatives can be ranked.

The result of ranking alternative analyses of costs in relationship to effective program results is cost-benefit determination. That is, cost benefit is the accrued value of the least expensive, most effective program outcome in terms of all resource allocations, looking both at accomplishing objectives and assessing consequences. Chapter

Eight of this volume proposes some possible cost benefits for institutions that utilize some different management techniques for achieving their current educational objectives. Cost benefits may be described in terms of long-term benefit to society, immediate effectiveness of the program for students enrolled, or simply the alternatives which rank at the top of any list of methods of achieving the same outcomes with a variety of resource allocations and related costs.

Cost analysis is essentially a six-step procedure which begins by collecting and grouping all direct resources and related dollar costs reduced to the smallest unit of measure applicable to the program being studied. Departments, administrative units such as the admissions office, or any individual program can be analyzed depending upon the ability of persons doing the cost accounting to understand all the direct resources that go into that program operation and to perceive a true dollar value for each of the resources.

Some resources which are utilized do not have dollar values and must be treated separately. For example, in an analysis of the effectiveness of a department of physics, one Ph.D. in physics may be a better teacher than another Ph.D. in physics even though both teachers receive the same salary. For these two faculty members the cost allocation would be the same, but the resource input would vary considerably. Colleges are not always able to reward the quality of instruction in such a way that the difference would be evident in determining the cost of the program until the replacement of the more able teacher is required and two people are necessary to do the work of one.

The process of collecting and grouping direct costs is quite difficult. Program budgeting is a great asset to cost accounting because it is a comprehensive attempt to treat all costs related to all programs in the institution in the same fashion and leads immediately into evaluation of effectiveness of programs. Indirect or constant costs—such as administrative expenditures, maintenance, student services, and library technical services—are usually allocated by formula or divided equally among departments or program units. It is just as well to leave out indirect costs altogether in computations in cost accounting if the indirect costs are going to be divided equally among all units in the institutions to be compared.

The second step is to examine output or accomplishment of

objectives of the unit being measured. This may mean restating present goals in terms that are more measurable or at least more assessable. For example, if the physics department is being evaluated, its service function may be lost if the only objective considered is to produce majors who score 500 on the Undergraduate Record Examination. The value of a physics department to the community outside the institution, particularly if it operates an observatory, may not be immediately included in traditional objectives. So a careful examination is necessary of the extent to which objectives are accomplished and their consequences understood.

The third step ties together steps 1 and 2, relating the resources and their dollar value to the outcomes or the extent of accomplishment of objectives determined for the program unit. Thus, the physics department in the preceding illustration would be evaluated on the relationship between the resources allocated and the extent to which it accomplished its objectives.

Just as input and output can be compared in one department or program unit, the ratio of resources to outcomes can be compared from one institution to another or from one department to another within the same institution if the objectives are relatively the same. Thus, if it costs $1000 a year to produce a chemistry graduate, $2000 a year to produce a physics graduate, and $500 a year to produce a social science graduate in any field in that area, the institution is able to rank all the departments on the relationship of resource allocation to outcome or in terms of input and output. The rank order may change when other factors, such as consequences of programs, are added as a part of the resource output.

The fifth step is to acknowledge those programs with the greatest and the least cost benefit based on ranking, either from one institution to another or within a single institution or between alternative methods of achieving the same outcome for different dollar values in the same program unit. This fifth step is more a conclusion reached than an actual procedure to be followed.

Once the various methods of analyzing a program unit have been carried out and the cost benefits determined, the sixth and most obvious step is to implement the least expensive procedure for achieving the desired objectives, so that the theoretical cost benefit can become a real benefit to the institution. Cost-effectiveness analysis would suggest that large classes are more economical than small classes that produce the same cognitive results. Thus, the cost benefit is the dollars saved by developing more large classes and reducing the number of faculty without producing less learning. When cost-effectiveness analysis is carried out for a program unit over a period of years, it is possible to experiment with a variety of procedures for achieving an objective and ultimately to settle on the method which produces the greatest cost benefit.

There are many problems with cost analysis which remain to be solved by those willing to attempt it. It is by no means a clearly understood or even uniformly practiced activity in higher educational management. One of the most pressing problems is the lack of a fully developed methodology for resource and cost analysis. Higher education has to draw on other disciplines and techniques from a number of the social sciences to carry out any effective cost analysis program.

The determination of costs for resources that normally do not have dollar values is also an extremely difficult process. Measuring the effectiveness of program units is likewise a difficult task, partly because higher educationists have not been willing to do so in the past and consequently do not have the instruments available and partly because colleges do not clearly define and agree upon the activities they are assessing. Until they do agree internally, no one can possibly assess their effectiveness.

A single measure, such as the relationship of input to output or a cost-benefit figure, is an inadequate way of expressing the relationships of many complex factors, and any cost analysis statement requires a number of if-then phrases to accompany it. A single dollar cost per student graduate in physics, for example, conceals much of the information needed for decision making about other aspects of the physics program and its cost benefit to the community, to other departments in the institution, or to alumni who may contribute large sums to their alma mater.

Finally, a methodology for estimating the effectiveness of future programs without going through the process of experimenting has yet to be determined. Colleges must rely on what other institutions have already experimented with or go through the painful and extensive process of trying out a number of alternative methods for achieving objectives. A great deal of this can be done by guess, by intuition, by observation, by comparison with other institutions. In the long run the need is deep for formulas and methodologies that allow for projection of costs in relationship to effectiveness.

For those willing to try it, cost analysis, although an incomplete and complex process, can be a very meaningful management tool in long-range planning. The procedures can be simplified; more answers can be estimated rather than absolutely determined. With resources such as those in this volume, institutions can benefit from cost analysis much more readily. Cost analysis leads directly into a planning strategy.

Strategy Applied

A college administrator or faculty member interested in applying the cost analysis strategy outlined in this chapter can do so by following several steps, leading to the production of tables found in Chapters Two and Three. The first step is to *gather the necessary information* from the college records for the last complete year. All terms in the regular academic year should be included but summer school excluded if faculty are paid extra for it. The analysis includes a full year of financial and academic data. Put all data onto forms found at the end of this chapter, following the directions for each form. No additional information should be needed. The second step in cost analysis is *tabulation of data collected*. This section describes the way to prepare the tables developed in the comparative analysis of colleges for the Council for the Advancement of Small Colleges. Samples of necessary tables are provided.

The third step is *data analysis*—reading the tables compiled in step 2. Guidance can be found in Chapters Two, Three, and Four, which analyze the normative data for the colleges in this study and suggest their meaning. The final step is the implemented judgment that readers of the data make about the relationship of cost to quality—that is, *cost effectiveness*. Guidance for this step can be found in Chapter Five.

Table 25 shows the form for determining distribution of staff and student time by class size. To complete this form, three variables must be extracted from Form 2 (see Forms 1–6 at end of this chapter). They are class size (determined by student enrollment in the given class), teacher credit hours (or the credit hours which a single student obtains upon successful completion of the class), and student credit hours (computed by multiplying the number of students in a given class by the teacher credit hours for the class). Class size is the basic variable for this table.

The distribution is derived by tallying the number of classes

Table 25.

DISTRIBUTION OF STAFF AND STUDENT TIME BY CLASS SIZE

FIRST SEMESTER

College .... Year ....

Class Size	Number of Courses	Total Teacher Credit Hours	% of Teacher Credit Hours	Total Student Credit Hours	% of Student Credit Hours
1– 5					
6–10					
11–15					
16–20					
21–25					
26–30					
31–35					
36–40					
41–45					
46–50					
Over 50					
Total					

Average Class Size

within each class-size range. The concomitant variables of teacher credit hours and student credit hours should be tallied in accordance with their class-size distribution. Use one copy of the form for a rough tally and another for a summary with percents added.

Of special significance here is the caution to include every fall-semester class listed on Form 2. The total number of classes, teacher credit hours, and student credit hours will be consistent with later tables.

Compute the percentage columns by reference to the columns headed "Teacher Credit Hours" and "Student Credit Hours" (in Form 2). Divide the figure in each class-size range by the total figure found at the bottom of the appropriate column. Enter the result in the proper class-size range in the appropriate percentage column, whether the reference is to teacher or student credit hours. The total of the percentages in each column should, of course, equal 100 percent. This chart is completed by determining average class size. To do so, divide the total number of teacher credit hours into the total student credit hours.

The distribution shown in Table 26 is based primarily upon the variable "number of teacher credit hours taught by a given teacher during the first semester." It is charted by first listing on a separate sheet all teachers who actually taught in the semester being studied and then determining the number of course credit hours that each one taught. These credit hours should be listed by subject after the teacher's name (in the event that the teacher is active in several distinct subject areas). On another separate sheet, all teachers in each subject should be listed—that is, grouped according to subject taught.

In the form shown in Table 26, the concept of full-time-equivalent (FTE) faculty is critical. This concept is based upon the number of hours taught by a given teacher or, in some instances, that part of his total work assignable to teaching. An institution has already determined on Form 1 whether the teacher is full time (1.00 FTE) or part time (a fraction of 1.00 FTE). It is, of course, the institution's prerogative to determine the procedure for computing the exact fractional equivalent involved in part-time equivalency. One commonly used practice is to divide the credit-hour figure which is realized as the average teaching load of all full-time teachers into

Table 26.

DISTRIBUTION OF TEACHING LOAD

FIRST SEMESTER

College .... Year ....

Number of Teacher Credit Hours	Number of Teachers	Total Teacher Credit Hours	Percent of Teachers
Under 7			
7– 8.9			
9–10.9			
11–12.9			
13–14.9			
15–16.9			
17–18.9			
19 and Over			
Total			

Average Teaching Load

the actual number of credit hours a given part-time teacher teaches. The resulting percentage is the part-time equivalency. In other cases, however, when the same teacher combines teaching with administration, a salary ratio may be more appropriate. Of course, some teachers may carry less than the average credit-hour load and still be considered full time. A third way of computing is to use twelve hours as full time and divide all part-time hours by 12 when a college is on the semester system.

The final step, after determining the number of credit hours each teacher teaches, is to set down the full- or part-time equivalency in numerical equivalents for each teacher. To form the distribution, simply indicate, in the column headed "Number of Teachers," the number of teachers who taught, for instance, 7–8.9 actual teacher credit hours, and so on. The credit-hour ranges will determine where the tallies for number of teachers and for total teacher credit hours will be placed. The tallies for number of teachers will be in terms of full- or part-time equivalency (as indicated in Form 1). Therefore, if a teacher is listed as full time, a tally of 1 is indicated. If half time, a tally of .5 would be correct. The total for the "Number of Teachers" column will equal the total FTE faculty for the college.

The "Total Teacher Credit Hours" column is the accumulated tallies of teacher credit hours, credit hours which belong to all the individual teachers tallied in the preceding column. The total for this teacher credit-hour column must equal its sister column in Table 25.

The last column, "Percent of Teachers," is computed by referring back to the "Number of Teachers" column. The percent of teachers for each line on the chart is figured by dividing the total number of teachers (or total FTE) into the number of teachers (or FTE) within each credit-hour range. The resulting percentages for each range, when totaled, should equal 100 percent.

The chart is completed by dividing total number of teacher credit hours by the total number of teachers to obtain the average teaching load. This figure will be used as a checkpoint with the figure shown in Table 27 (grand total of column "Load by Teacher Credit Hours").

Table 27 is the first of two summary charts which have the subject areas as the major category. The initial step in completing this summary is to determine the number of FTE teachers in each subject area. This procedure is aided if the procedure suggested for Table 26 (arranging teachers and credit hours according to subject taught) has been followed.

The determination of FTE for a subject area (for instance, biology) is easy if all teachers of biology courses teach only biology. The FTE computation is more difficult if some teachers teach in more than one department. In this case, a ratio must be developed which reflects the proportion of the various subject areas in the teacher's full- or part-time equivalency. The sum of the FTE fractions generated by a single teacher for several subject areas must equal that teacher's original full-time equivalency, whether it be full time or fractional. Thus, if a full-time teacher teaches six hours of biology, three hours of chemistry, and three hours of physics, biology would be .5 and each of the others .25.

Once each teacher's FTE total has been accounted for in the appropriate subject sector, these figures should be totaled and entered on the chart in the first column. The grand-total figure should equal the total number of teachers shown in Table 26.

The next column, "Load by Number of Courses," is figured by first grouping all first-semester classes and sections (listed on Form 2) into their appropriate subject area, adding them by area, and entering the sums on the chart.

Once this process has been completed, the final figures for the subject areas may be computed. To do this, first sum the FTE figures to the grand-total stage. The sums and individual subject-area addends will be used henceforth as divisors in computing the final figures for columns 2, 3, and 4 of this chart.

The third column, "Load by Teacher Credit Hours," is a two-step procedure. The first step refers to the already grouped classes by subject area and involves summing the teacher credit-hour figures (found in column 4 of Form 2) for each subject taught during the first semester. The last column, "Load by Student Credit Hours," is also a two-step procedure. First, the student credit hours (found in column 6 of Form 2) for each subject taught during the first semester are added. Once this step has been accomplished for both columns, all these tentatively entered figures and subtotals should be divided by the FTE divisor for that subject, subtotal or total line. This second step for columns 2, 3, and 4 on this chart involves division and not addition. Addition *is* involved in arranging the totals, subtotals, and grand totals of information from Form 2 for the first step. Adherence to this procedure will curtail any erroneous tendency to "average averages."

When, in this final step, the FTE faculty figure is divided into the corresponding figures in the course, credit-hour, and student-credit-hour columns, the FTE divisor may be less than 1.00 in certain subject areas. In this case, the fractional FTE divisor should assume the value of 1 for purposes of the computation only. Dividing by 1 will ensure that the resulting loads will be realistic and consistent.

Table 27.

SUMMARY OF FACULTY TEACHING LOAD

FIRST SEMESTER

College .... Year ....

Subject	Number of FTE Teachers	Load by Number of Courses	Load by Teacher Credit Hours	Load by Student Credit Hours
Natural Sciences				
Biology				
Chemistry				
Geology				
Mathematics				
Physical Sci.				
Physics				
Other				
Total				
Social Sciences				
Economics				
History				
Political Sci.				
Psychology				
Social Sci.				
Sociology				
Social Welfare				
Other				
Total				
Humanities				
Art				
Drama				
English				
French				

Subject	Number of FTE Teachers	Load by Number of Courses	Load by Teacher Credit Hours	Load by Student Credit Hours
Humanities (Con't)				
German				
Greek				
Humanities				
Latin				
Music				
Philosophy				
Religion				
Spanish				
Speech				
Other				
Total				
Professional				
Accounting				
Business				
Education				
Engineering				
Home Ec.				
Journalism				
Medical Tech.				
Nursing				
Other				
Total				
Subtotal				
Physical Ed.				
Grand Total				

Table 27 provides two checkpoints for the analysis. The grand totals for the columns "Number of Courses," "Teacher Credit Hours," and "Student Credit Hours" should equal the corresponding columns in Table 25 before they are divided by the FTE teacher total to determine the average loads by course, credit hour, and student credit hour. Another checkpoint is found by comparing the final, divided grand-total figure in column 3, "Load by Teacher Credit Hours," with the figure for "Average Teaching Load" shown in Table 26. These two figures should be identical.

Table 28 is the second summary chart involving the subject areas. Completion of this chart involves only addition. Success is dependent upon careful grouping of courses from Form 2 (both semesters). Column 1, "Number of FTE Teachers" (first semester), is copied from column 1 in Table 27.

Column 2, "Number of Different Courses," is determined in three steps. First, the number of different courses in the first semester in each subject area should be ascertained. A course is different if its actual content is different. Sections, laboratories, or different classes of the same course would not be considered different even if offered in another semester of the same year. The second step applies the same procedure and criteria to the second semester. The last stage involves comparing the resultant different courses of each semester to insure that only different courses are tallied for the whole academic year in each subject area. Thus, English 101 taught each semester would be counted only once. The totals of this column are then added.

Column 3, "Majors," is completed by referring to the corresponding subject areas listed on Form 3 (at end of chapter) and filling in the appropriate subject. The various totals are added. Figures for each subject area are determined by adding *all* declared majors from freshmen through seniors for each subject.

The "Total Teacher Credit Hours" column is computed by summing the total credit hours taught in each semester or term of the academic year and adding the resulting totals for each subject area. The total for the initial semester is already available, of course, in Table 26. The total hours for the second semester are gathered from Form 2. January terms are added with the second semester.

The last column of this table, "Total Student Credit Hours," is computed in the same general manner as the preceding column ("Teacher Credit Hours") for the entire academic year. The totals, subtotals, and grand totals of this column, as well as this whole summary table, involve only addition.

Table 29, the form for tabulating Comparison of Averages, involves computation of indices which are felt to be significant in evaluating an institution's efficiency on an interinstitutional comparative basis. Line 1 of this chart (enrollment) is the total figure from Form 5. This figure is especially salient in viewing institutions comparatively and also as a basis for future computations on this chart.

Line 2, total FTE faculty, may be taken from the totals in Table 26 under the column "Number of Teachers." This figure is used as a basis for determining the various averages which appear later on this chart.

Line 3, average class size, is available from Table 25 (last line).

The bottom figure in Table 26 yields line 4, average teaching load (in credit hours).

Line 5, average productivity (in student credit hours), refers to faculty production and is determined by dividing the total FTE faculty figure into the total number of student credit hours for the academic year. The total FTE figure is, of course, the same as entered on line 2 of this chart. The student-credit-hour figure for the whole year is available from Table 28 (grand-total line under the column "Total Student Credit Hours").

The average student-credit-hour load (first semester) is found by obtaining the total student credit hours from Table 25 and dividing the student enrollment figure on line 1 into it. This average, entered on line 6, represents a student average as opposed to the faculty average on line 5.

The faculty-student ratio (first semester) is computed by dividing line 2 (FTE faculty) into line 1 (college enrollment).

Lines 8, 9, and 10 are derived from Form 1. Line 8, average FTE faculty cash salary, is computed in two steps: sum the cash-salary column of Form 1 and divide this total by the total FTE faculty figure. Line 9 involves summation of the benefits column of Form 1 for all faculty listed and then dividing this sum by the same

Table 28.

SUMMARY BY SUBJECTS

College .... Year ....

Subject	Number of FTE[a] Teachers	Number of Different Courses	Majors	Total Teacher Credit Hours	Total Student Credit Hours
Natural Sciences					
Biology					
Chemistry					
Geology					
Mathematics					
Natural Sci.					
Physical Sci.					
Physics					
Other					
Total					
Social Sciences					
Economics					
History					
Political Sci.					
Psychology					
Social Sci.					
Sociology					
Social Welfare					
Other					
Total					
Humanities					
Art					
Drama					
English					
French					

Subject	Number of FTE[a] Teachers	Number of Different Courses	Majors	Total Teacher Credit Hours	Total Student Credit Hours
Humanities (Cont'd)					
German					
Greek					
Humanities					
Latin					
Music					
Philosophy					
Religion					
Spanish					
Speech					
Other					
Total					
Professional					
Accounting					
Business					
Education					
Engineering					
Home Ec.					
Journalism					
Medical Tech.					
Nursing					
Other					
Total					
Subtotal					
Physical Ed.					
Grand Total					

[a] Full-time equivalent for fall semester only.

Table 29.

COMPARISON OF AVERAGES

College .... Year ....

1. College enrollment	
2. Full-time-equivalent faculty	
3. Average class size	
4. Average teaching load (in credit hours)	
5. Average productivity (in student credit hours)	
6. Average student credit-hour load (1st semester)	
7. Faculty-student ratio (1st semester)	
8. Average FTE faculty cash salary	
9. Average FTE faculty benefits	
10. Average FTE total faculty salary	
11. Overhead ratio on faculty salary	
12. Average cost per student	
13. Average income per student (tuition and all fees)	
14. Total educational expenditure	
15. Total income from tuition and fees	
16. Percent of expenditure borne by tuition and fees[a]	

[a] Excludes unfunded scholarships.

FTE faculty figure. Line 10 is, of course, the sum of lines 8 and 9. For those institutions concerned with salaries regarded as "contributed services," these services should be established at a specific money figure and added in the conventional manner.

Line 11 (overhead ratio) is determined through treatment of two figures: educational and general expenditure (found on Form 6) and total faculty compensation (last column on Form 1). The faculty compensation figure is subtracted from the educational and general expenditure figure, and the difference is divided by the total faculty compensation figure. This ratio is then entered on line 11 and provides a picture of the part which faculty salary plays in the total expenditure process of an institution.

Line 12, average cost per student, is computed by dividing college enrollment into the educational and general expenditure figure from Form 6.

Average income per student, line 13, provides a sound comparison with the average cost figure on the preceding line. This average is computed by extracting the figure for student fees (under educational and general income on Form 6) and dividing it by total FTE student enrollment.

Line 14, total educational expenditure, is taken from Form 6. It is, of course, the same figure utilized in computing lines 11 and 12.

Line 15, total income from tuition and fees, is computed by referring to Form 6. This entry was used for line 13.

The final line, percent of expenditure borne by tuition and fees, is computed by a two-step process. Subtract all unfunded student aid from the student fees income figure on Form 6. Divide the resultant difference into total educational and general expenditure (line 14 above) for the percentage of actual expenses paid for by students from outside funds.

Another table (not shown here) could be prepared listing the cost of faculty time per student credit hour. First, list all subjects or departments of the college in the left column. In the second column put the result of dividing total faculty compensation for that academic year in a given subject by the total number of student credit hours taught in all terms of the academic year in the same subject. Faculty salary for each subject is determined from Form 1. Add the total compensation of all full-time and part-time teachers in a subject to the proportionate share of the salaries of teachers who divide their salary between subjects or between teaching and administration. The figure is then divided by the total student credit hours taught in all terms of the academic year; student credit hours are extracted from each subject line of column 4 in Table 28. Thus, a total faculty salary of $10,000 in art at College X is divided by the total hours of art taught (which was 100) for a faculty cost per credit hour of $100.

Another figure that can be derived from these data is total direct cost per credit hour—the sum of faculty salaries by subject and departmental costs divided by total student credit hours by subject. A column for this figure could be added to the preceding Faculty Cost chart. The total direct-cost figure is determined by taking the faculty salary figure by subject (determined in the preceding chart) and adding to it the departmental or subject costs found on Form 4. If the academic department combines more than one subject area, add all appropriate faculty salaries. Divide the sum just determined by the total student credit hours taught by subject (column 4 in Table 28). The resultant dollar figure is the total direct cost per credit hour by subject or department. It does not include indirect costs of administration, utilities and maintenance.

Finally, various financial charts can be compiled. These charts are a direct transfer from Form 6, where institutional financial data are listed. No tabulations are necessary.

Planning Strategy

What areas should a long-range plan include? The whole program of an institution should be covered, including the college philosophy, structural organization, facilities, faculty, curriculum, finances, and students. These are the seven components of higher education. They are inclusive and can be fitted together in varying amounts. Philosophy is the way of educating, structure is the form of educating, students are the persons educated, faculty are the persons educating, curriculum is the educational program and materials, facilities are the place for educating, and finance is the support for education.

This total educational program includes the way in which it

is administered and the way it relates to the community. Church affiliations, federal governmental relationships, professional associations, accrediting associations, all the communities or public of an institution must be considered, since in reality they often determine the shape and scope of programs more than do the internal operations. What the government wants has been for many institutions the guide for charting their long-range plans. The government is gentle compared to the way in which some private foundations structure a college program. But the whole community must be included.

What does long-range planning involve? First of all, it must be for continuous change, not just for a single attempt at upgrading, though that is helpful. The plan must be structured so that each year it can be reviewed by the faculty and the administration and revised or restructured in light of new evidence.

The long-range plan should probably extend for five years generally and three years specifically. That is, a college should sight the general direction and major goals for five years, concentrate on a specific plan for three years, and plan in full detail for two years. Each year the institution should add a year to its plan, so that it is always five years ahead.

Long-range planning should involve the best personnel available in the college. The most alert individuals need to be included in order for the best plan to emerge. These persons should not be directly responsible for implementing the plans they make. If the people who do the real master planning can be in a position to plan, chart, and recommend but separated from the necessity of implementing decisions, their creativity is less likely to be hampered. Administrators can implement the ideas of the planners.

The master planning committee could utilize an assistant to the president as coordinator. The committee should also include the institutional researcher, some department or division chairmen or their representative, selected faculty representation at large, and students, alumni, or trustees. No more than twelve people, however, should be on the committee.

Another possibility is to use the president's committee on policy, program, and budget if he has such an advisory committee already constituted from among the faculty. Yet another is to let the long-range plan be conducted entirely by the institutional researchers.

Planning groups need to be trained, but proper training is not offered anywhere in the United States, even at a professional level. There are some places—for instance, at Michigan State under Paul Dressel—where individuals can be apprentices; and there are a few short courses in long-range planning and institutional analysis. Books and planning resources can give guidance, but the committee and the faculty have to educate themselves, doing a lot of guesswork in the process. The planning manual prepared by the National Association of College and University Business Officers is one of the best guides for an inexperienced team working without a computer.

Long-range planning must be conducted in each unit of the college in the same way that the master plan develops. The chaplain's office, the student affairs office, the admissions office, the department or division—each small unit where any responsibility resides within the institution must make its own plan.

Unit plans are given to the master planning committee. Everybody has a chance to prepare the plan in the area in which he is most knowledgeable and most responsible. Each unit of the college should have a planning coordinator who is not the administrator of the department or the plant manager, but someone close to him, and who can be freed to spend more of his time on planning than can other members of that unit.

With which of the seven components (philosophy, organization, facilities, faculty curriculum, finances, students) does planning begin? Sound long-range planning starts with the educational program, since that is the main business of the college; community service and research, to the extent that they exist, grow out of it. Campus plans, financial projections, and enrollment projections all must be determined by the educational program plans and decisions, or else the master plan will be unrelated to the functions of the college.

How does a college start a long-range plan? One way is to begin with a statement of assumptions establishing the framework for looking at everything the institution does. In most colleges there is no consensus about the assumptions that supposedly underlie practices, because faculty and staff perceive the environment differently or do not understand the difference between assumptions and goals or purposes. Assumptions differ from the goals of an institution in that they describe conditions which cannot be markedly affected. They constitute institutional "givens." The assumptions are religious, economic, sociopolitical, and educational in nature, and international, national, regional, and local in purview. What will be the religious climate, the economic situation, the sociopolitical temperature, and the educational viewpoint in the college town, the county, the state, and America in five years? Answers to each piece of that question undergird a long-range plan.

After assessing external assumptions, a college must determine its goals in light of them. Goals demonstrate the conviction of change and purposeful progress, and colleges which have not cited goals in terms of the social environment have progressed haphazardly.

Historically colleges have grown up piecemeal. Each new idea that has come along has been attached to what was already being done, resulting in a great hodgepodge of activities and functions. When community service was the fashion, colleges added programs that did everything but deliver groceries; when research was the fashion, colleges added all kinds of institutes and centers; the current rage is for computers, programmed learning devices, and audiovisual experts. In the middle of all this, nobody has remembered what the institution set out to do or why it was chartered. College buildings get built the same way, depending more on what the traffic will bear and the government will buy than on what the institution needs to support its educational program effectively.

The goals of an institution of higher learning focus upon three areas—instruction, research, and service—as they relate to the mission of the college. All data collected and assessed now feed into the process of setting goals. These data must be matched or cross-referenced to guarantee full coverage of all forces and counterforces. The committee uses the cost analyses to form the value judgments they set forth as goals and as a rationale for or defense of the goals as well.

After the goals have been established, the same committee can proceed to develop the long-range plan. The plan depends upon the data analysis and the institutional goals. Growing out of the goals, the plan amounts to an implementation of them, a functional means to secure their achievement. According to the earlier definition, the committee must determine, in light of the goals, what the college will need in two, three, and five years in terms of facilities, faculties, students, organization, and curriculum. The committee next must determine the resources necessary to achieve the goals and fulfill the needs, and finally it must make a systematic plan to move step by step toward achievement.

Advantages and Disadvantages

There are several disadvantages to long-range planning which should be remembered as planning progresses. Tensions always exist which lead to short tempers and resistance to change as soon as an encompassing plan is undertaken by an institution. By careful selection of committees, some inertia can be bypassed and rebels involved in constructive leadership of the project.

Comprehensive plans place limitations upon individual operations. As the college develops a plan, independent activity is limited and directed; individuals are no longer able to go off on tangents, adding five or six courses in their departments, shifting the emphasis of their programs, or engaging in any number of activities that they might desire because of professional training and temperament. This restriction sometimes is a disadvantage because a lot of individual creativity may be stifled unless continuous change is possible within the plan developed.

A long-range plan is bound to benefit some individuals and disadvantage others. Some programs are going to be enhanced and others are going to be restricted. When planning begins, all faculty and staff need to understand this and know that, as they plan, they must first have the whole institution and the students in mind, and last of all their own program and vested interests.

There are, however, more advantages than disadvantages to long-range planning. First of all, a plan forces an institution to make public decisions on major matters. Every prospective faculty member knows in advance what the focus, purpose, and direction of the college will be. Such a situation is comforting, if nothing else, though an individual may not agree with it.

Long-range plans work to overcome stagnation. Every year the whole program of the institution is reevaluated, making it impossible for a person to sit quietly by for very long in any given area and let the waters flow over him.

Planning points out the weaknesses in an institution—weakness that might otherwise be covered up, deliberately or unintentionally. When people work in a place for a long time, they overlook many things that go on. They no longer see any problem areas because they have lived with these weaknesses for so long. But a plan brings problems out into the open, focuses attention systematically upon the institution, and brings everybody to a similar understanding of the assumptions and goals.

Also, long-range planning helps to promote realism and to avoid fantasy idealism, not genuine idealism but tangential idealism, and helps to keep faculty and staff firmly anchored to the plan and to the program.

The plan helps to explain in objective dollar-and-cents terms the reasons for administrative positions. The greatest help an administrator can have if he has to make faculty salary adjustments, tuition adjustments, or other decisions that are hard to make in an institution is a long-range plan in which everyone has participated. They know that when he says, "This is what we are going to have to do and this is why," he is not the "mean old man" who runs the college by fiat.

The process of long-range planning is probably more valuable than the results. Participation, working through in one's own mind and with others, giving and taking, compromising, and finally reaching tenable positions is the most valuable part of a long-range plan. For the greatest degree of fulfillment most of the people involved must be at the institution through the whole planning process and the implementation of the plan, but even to have gone through the experience for a part of the time is worthwhile.

Finally, and most important, a long-range plan makes a college a model of what it tries to inculcate in its graduates: the ability to make planned, consciously understood choices in the best interests of all involved for the common good.

Data-Collection Forms

The following forms are necessary for a small college to do the basic institutional self-study described. Examples of the needed forms, along with descriptions of the data-gathering methodology, are provided here.

Form 1—Faculty salary. List all faculty alphabetically (full time and part time) by subject, giving their cash salary and benefits separately. Check whether they are full time or part time. For all part-time faculty list what percentage of a full-time-equivalent faculty they are on your records. If you have faculty who are contributing their salary, list the equivalent salary they would be paid for their rank and position. If you have administrators who also teach, list only that portion of their salary which is paid to them for their teaching function—and list under part-time faculty the percent of their faculty teaching equivalent.

Form 2—Courses. List all courses taught—by section (each section written separately whether or not it was taught by the same faculty member) and alphabetically by subject area (art, biology, business, etc.). For all courses list what is considered by your college to be the teacher credit load under "Teacher Credit Hours," followed by enrollment; these two figures are multiplied to give the "Student Credit Hours" figure. All laboratory sections, individual miscellaneous sections, and physical education sections must be listed in this way in order to obtain an accurate picture of where faculty time and student time are being spent. All sections must be listed separately and alphabetically by subject area. All subjects, whether or not the student receives credit for them, must be cited and must have a figure under "Teacher Credit Hours" in order to know where faculty time is spent. Zero credit courses need to be given a value of 1 in order to compute student credit hours if the college has no other designation for faculty for these courses. Colleges on the quarter system should follow these same directions, however, if you wish to be compared with schools on the semester system, convert your figures to semester hours. If you wish to be compared to other quarter colleges, leave your figures as they are and follow the directions—substituting quarter where semester appears on forms and charts.

Form 3—Majors. List majors by the appropriate subject area alphabetically.

Form 4—Expenditure. List all administrative expenses by subject alphabetically. Include laboratory costs and material costs. (See bottom of form.)

Form 5—Enrollment. This form is self-explanatory.

Form 6—Income and expenditure. Please note the following points: (1) If possible, this form should be filled in by the business office from the annual audit. If the audit does not break out some categories listed, the audited figures should be divided. (2) The manual published by the Office of Administrative Services in Higher Education (State Education Department, Albany, New York) is the primary source of information for grouping items of expenditure and income. A useful supplement is the American Council's *College and University Business Administration.* Where these do not readily answer questions, the *Sixty College Study* (see bibliography) will be the third resource. (3) Intercollegiate athletic expenses should not be included in the Educational and General budget. All credit courses, of course, are included in the instructional program. (4) Debt retirement should not be included in the Educational and General budget but with other expenditures. Debt retirement on auxiliaries should be included in Auxiliaries. (5) Separate all public relations and development expenses from General Institutional. (6) Ordinarily the academic dean and his offices will be in the area of General Administration. If the dean teaches, that portion of his salary will be under Instructional Salaries. (7) All student fees will be recorded in the Educational and General income. (8) Some colleges have extensive off-campus programs involving choirs, bands, and the like. Any net income would be included under Income, and any net expense would be under Development.

Form 1.

FACULTY SALARY BY SUBJECT[a]

Name of College						Year
Name	Rank	Full or Part Time[b]	Cash Salary	Benefits		Total Compensation

[a] List all faculty alphabetically within each subject field. List faculty who teach in more than one department in the subject of greatest number of hours taught.
[b] If part time indicate the percent.

Form 2.

CLASSES TAUGHT

Name of College

Fall or Spring .... Semester[a] .... Year

Course Title[b] (include all sections)	Catalog Course No.	Professor's Name	Teacher Credit Hours	Students Enrolled	Student Credit Hours[e]

[a] List first semester separately from second semester. If you have terms other than two semesters in the regular academic year, include them all separately and label.
[b] List by subjects—all Art together, etc.
[e] Number of credit hours *times* number of students.

Form 3.

NUMBER OF DECLARED MAJORS[*]

Name of College   Year

Subject or Department	Seniors or Graduates in Current Year	Juniors in Current Year	Sophomores in Current Year	Freshmen or Others in Current Year

[*] Some students may be in combined subject departments or divisions; however, when majors can be listed by individual subject, the figures compare better with other colleges.

Form 4.

EXPENDITURE BY ACADEMIC DEPARTMENT[a]

Name of College	Year

Name of Department	Total Expenditures for Year

[a] Exclude faculty salaries but include faculty travel (if not counted as a fringe benefit), student help actually paid by the college (portion of work-study), supplies, noncapital equipment, and any other departmental expenditure. When these figures can be compiled for individual subject areas, they compare best with other colleges.

Form 5.

FULL-TIME-EQUIVALENT ENROLLMENT[a]

Name of College					Year
Fall Semester		*Spring Semester*		*Other Terms*[b]	
Full-Time Enrollment	Part-Time Equivalent	Full-Time Enrollment	Part-Time Equivalent	Full-Time Enrollment	Part-Time Equivalent

[a] Indicate full-time enrollment in student body count and part-time enrollment by totaling credit hours taken by part-time students and dividing by 12.
[b] Indicate third semester, interterm, etc.

Form 6.

Income and Expenditure

College ....

Name of Respondent ....

Date: ....

Year: ....

Current Income: Educational and General	$	%
A. Student Fees (tuition and all fees)	....	....
B. Government Appropriations	....	....
C. Endowment	....	....
D. Gifts and Grants (excluding government grants)	....	....
E. Contributed Services (net)	....	....
F. Sponsored Research	....	....
G. Other Separately Budgeted Research	....	....
H. Other Sponsored Programs	....	....
I. Organized Activities	....	....
J. Miscellaneous	....	....
Total Educational and General	....	100%

Summary of All Income	$	%
I. Educational and General	....	....
II. Auxiliary	....	....
III. Student Aid (excluding loan funds, including government grants)	....	....
IV. Other Educational Operations	....	....
V. Intercollegiate Athletics	....	....
Total Current Income	....	....
Total Current Expenditures	....	....
Excess Current Income over Current Expenditures	....	....
VI. Capital Gifts	....	....
A. Endowment	....	....
B. Plant or Permanent Equipment	....	....
C. Annuities and Deferred Gifts Not Used for Current Income	....	....
Total Capital Gifts	....	100%

Current Expenditures: Educational and General ....

  A. Instructional Salaries ....

  B. Instructional Supplies and Expense ....

  C. Organized Activities ....

  D. Sponsored Research ....

  E. Other Separately Budgeted Research ....

  F. Other Sponsored Programs ....

  G. Libraries ....

  H. Student Services ....

  I. Operations and Maintenance ....

  J. General Administration ....

  K. Staff Benefits (excluding faculty) ....

  L. Faculty Benefits ....

  M. Development (take out of General
     Institutional) ....

  N. General Institutional ....

    Total Educational and General 100%

Summary of all Expenditures $ %

  I. Educational and General ....

  II. Auxiliary Enterprises ....

  III. Student Aid ....

  IV. Intercollegiate Athletics ....

  V. Debt Service ....
    Total Current Expenditures 100%

Chapter VIII

❧❧❧❦❦❦

Recommendations for Effectiveness

College catalogs are notorious for the way in which their statements of purpose are phrased. Sometimes they are awesome; the purpose of one college, for instance, is "to bring the kingdom of God to the campus"—a laudable purpose but difficult to measure. Sometimes statements are clichés like "unique, meaningful experience." In almost all instances, purposes are phrased in vague generalities. Three of the most commonly stated purposes—growth, distinction, and

154

excellence—are closely allied with three of the most severe problems outlined in the preceding chapters.

Purposes and Problems

Most small liberal arts colleges desire to grow. Increase in numbers of students indicates a kind of quality; if more and more people want to attend the college, it must be a "good" college. Increase in numbers of students helps meet inflation. More students mean more staff and facilities and an expanded curriculum, so that the campus and the catalog "look like a real college on the move." In short, many small-college administrators see increased enrollment as the path away from a deficit operation and, consciously or subconsciously, make growth a primary purpose of their institutions.

Increased enrollment by itself, however, is part of the economic problem of the small college, not the solution. Unless or until students pay the full cost of their education, growth means greater expenditures, not savings. For every dollar brought to a college by increased numbers of students, the school has to find additional funds (anywhere from five cents to seventy cents, depending on the percentage of costs paid by students).

Neither cost per student nor income per student appeared to be related to institutional size in this analysis. Expenditures were unrelated to effectiveness as well. In one college increased enrollment may redeem a budget; in another it may lead to greater deficit. There is no reliable pattern of growth that can be coupled with increased efficiency. Theoretically at least, a college could become smaller and more economically managed if it could drop unneeded faculty, staff, and facilities.

The desire to be distinctive leads to a second major problem. Dollars are spent on projected rather than real growth. Colleges prepare thoughtful long-range plans, including all kinds of distinctive programs, predicated almost always on enrollment growth to sustain salary increases and rising costs. Once that pattern is established, it becomes evident that more resources and faculty will be needed if the college is to show good faith and be ready for the students. Contracts are issued for better-paid faculty and new materials a year in advance. If the students do not materialize, the college gets a deficit budget and a new admissions director.

The desire to be distinctive pressures the college to spend ahead of income in other ways as well. Faculty rightly say that it is difficult to get students into a program or department unless it is good. The problem lies in the definition of "good." Good is often measured in number of faculty, number of Ph.D.s, quality of facilities, amount of equipment, number of books in the library—all of which require advance expenditures. If "good department" could be defined by amount of learning of graduates, record of alumni in graduate school, ability of graduates to secure well-paying jobs, and satisfaction of graduates with the program, the dollar balance might be reversed and distinctiveness viewed as a by-product rather than a factor in input.

The desire to be excellent leads to a third serious problem. The mission of quality has always been laudable. No college would choose to be mediocre if it could be otherwise. A misunderstanding of the concept of excellence, however, produces the economic problem. Must a college offer an excellent program in every major liberal arts field in order to be a quality liberal arts college? Further, must a college offer every aspect of every field in order to be a quality liberal arts college?

Traditionally the answers have been yes. The practice of offering everything gets colleges in trouble. Selective excellence may produce more quality than trying to spread a limited number of dollars over many fields. Chemistry, physics, political science, art, drama, foreign languages, music, home economics, nursing, and physical education are the most expensive programs in liberal arts colleges. There are quality institutions in this nation which do not offer all these subjects. In fact, probably no one of these subjects is essential to liberal education.

If excellence is an absolute concept, the number of courses or amount of content necessary to produce a learned individual should be somewhat constant among institutions. But it is not. In colleges enrolling under 500 students, seven different chemistry courses a year produce a graduate; in colleges enrolling between 500 and 1000 students, it takes thirteen courses to produce roughly the same graduate. The range of different courses and different subjects offered among these colleges is large—causing expanded faculties, majors, and course offerings, and small classes and low faculty productivity. Yet, based on the assessment of the six colleges in Chapter Five, there is reason to believe that the colleges are not greatly disparate in their products, only in what they think necessary to produce their products—a great economic difference in understanding the concept of excellence.

Beyond the problems raised in this analysis, one other—studied in depth by William Jellema, formerly of the Association of American Colleges—deserves mention. In his follow-up study of 607 liberal arts colleges, Jellema discovered an actual average deficit of $131,000 in 1969–70, about 26 percent worse than anticipated, and a projected average deficit of $158,000 for 1970–71. "Behind these mounds of deficits lie the broken remains of curtailed operations, of abbreviated departments, of decimated academic programs, of faltering plans and languishing aspirations, of innovation untried and creativity curbed. . . . The number of institutions out of a total of 762 private accredited four-year colleges and universities in the nation that may be presumed on the basis of extrapolation from our study to have exhausted their liquid assets within ten years is 365—one for every day of the year. Instead of naming the days for the births of the saints, we can name them for the deaths of the colleges that are named for the saints" (Jellema, 1971b, pp. 2, 14).

To cite the inability to plan as the major cause of the present dilemma of the private liberal arts college is primarily to charge poor management. The present condition of these institutions is not necessarily the fault of poor management alone. Several other factors also account for their situation.

Causes of Problems

By and large, liberal arts colleges in America are based on outdated and inappropriate models, which restrict their efforts to find new, more efficient, and more effective forms. The university has been the model for governance. Departments, divisions, centers, institutes, faculty senates, and other governmental units necessitated by large size and complex systems do not have the same grounding or reason for existence in liberal arts colleges. Yet liberal arts institutions have rarely developed a form of of government reflecting their own size and purpose.

The economic model is equally inappropriate. In a period of declining enrollment and support, an economy based on increase is difficult to sustain. As yet no educational economy of equilibrium has been developed, but certainly such a design would be more appropriate to liberal education in the next decade or two.

The curriculum in most liberal arts colleges, well documented by Paul Dressel, Michael Brick, Earl McGrath, and others, has remained much the same for the last twenty years. This curriculum was probably appropriate for the kind of student then enrolled in liberal arts colleges (almost entirely from the top third of high school graduating classes), but it is out of date for nonselective institutions today.

Philosophically, liberal arts colleges are based on inappropriate models. For years a liberal education was assumed to be designed as a basis for preparing young people for effective citizenship in American society. That philosophic position began to change about five years ago. Increasingly, students want a career-oriented education. This new way of thinking about a college education challenges the philosophy, the curriculum, the structure, the policies, and the economics of most liberal arts colleges. In the next decade liberal education may appeal more to middle-aged persons, who have lived long enough to understand the value of liberal education, who want to be independent learners, who want a free spirit, who feel that they can take time to appreciate the world in which they live, and who want to learn to be wise. This shift in population will require a shift in philosophy which has not yet manifested itself in the behavior of most liberal arts colleges. Thus, in government, economics, curriculum, and philosophy these colleges tend to look to the wrong models.

That a liberal arts education is no longer a viable commodity is a frequently given reason for the present dilemma of liberal arts colleges. Larger numbers of economically lower-class and upper-lower-class citizens, as well as larger numbers of minorities, penetrate higher education; and an increasingly larger number of these people feel that a liberal arts education represents an "old value," belonging to the upper or upper-middle class and not particularly appropriate to an upward mobile, vocationally or professionally oriented population. Altogether, there is growing public disenchantment with high-cost, low-immediate-return "general education" in the liberal arts tradition and a growing enchantment with specialized professional training for immediate job placement.

Once the queen of higher education, private liberal arts colleges have now become second-choice institutions. They are often the learning ground for inexperienced administrators and faculty. Although education for citizenship is still considered an important national goal of postsecondary education, fewer and fewer citizens seem to believe that a liberal arts education is uniquely suited to produce a responsible citizen. But most of all, declining enrollment is evidence of a vote of no confidence in the private liberal arts college.

A number of uncontrollable factors, which lie to a large extent outside of education, are also responsible for part of the economic dilemma of private higher education and have caused management to respond to the society rather than initiate behavior of its own choosing. Howard Bowen (1972b, pp. 21–22) cites several of these. Labor legislation and the spread of collective bargaining in education have had a great impact on cost, particularly nonacademic personnel costs. Increases in construction and maintenance costs have been beyond the control of many colleges. Technological change requires colleges to buy expensive computers, microscopes, and other kinds of equipment necessary to prepare people for effective careers in growing industries. The proliferation of knowledge requires expanded acquisition of books and journals. The need to provide financial aid to a growing number of poor and underprepared students, who appeared in college after a radical shift in social concepts of who should be admitted, also became a major factor in increasing costs.

In addition to those factors cited by Bowen for all institutions, small private liberal arts colleges sometimes are an economic victim of their location. Because these colleges are frequently located away from sources of supply, transportation has generated extra costs; being located in the country has forced colleges to provide a variety of auxiliary services, such as health-care and student-activity programs, which schools in urban areas have not had to provide. Lower labor costs do not offset the cost of expensive unavailable specialists who must be imported to maintain a college campus.

In a decade of affluence, a number of liberal arts colleges dropped their religious affiliation or their ties with constituent groups of one kind or another. Now, when these affiliations are needed, the colleges find themselves with no one upon whom they can place a claim for students or dollars. In a sense, colleges brought these dilemmas of affiliation and location upon themselves, but in a time and under circumstances which could not be planned for or predicted.

The final major cause of the economic dilemma of the private college manifest in this study must be poor management. The small private liberal arts colleges of America, taken collectively, have not been well managed, but poor management is an easy charge to make as hindsight. More important, has any group of colleges been managed well enough to serve as a model for the private schools? No: the problem pervades all of American higher education. Was good management regarded as an important criterion in a decade of affluence? No: as the economy rose in the 1950s and 1960s and as the demand for higher education expanded, private colleges responded to the times. Management was a bad word. Administration was a service for faculty, who were to separate the able from the disabled learner and to produce the greatest quality possible, given the greatest quality of potential in incoming students. Only when the dollars are low and accountability high does the concept of management become critical. And once again, higher education is caught without a plan.

Although management has become an important concept, few places train managers. Most of the programs in higher education for administrators prepare them to work in two-year colleges; or, renouncing the practical concepts of management as inappropriate for graduate education, these programs are interested instead in preparing generalists, theorists, and professors who will preserve the current posture. The few places interested in training managers for all levels of administration in private higher education have not acquired sufficient status to be the hiring ground for the leaders of these institutions. Up through the ranks is still the pathway to management. Being a good teacher has been the primary criterion for being a good manager—a paradox that cheats students of good teaching *and* good management in their colleges. Poor management, the inability to plan, or the failure to recognize the need for efficiency and effectiveness cannot be blamed only on the president or the dean; the blame must be shared by the trustees, by other administrators, by the faculty, and, to a very great extent, by outside agencies such as accrediting associations and state and federal governments. These groups are part of the educational monolith that perpetuates assumptions, models, and management styles requiring obedience to established ways of administering and teaching in private higher education. In order to receive government dollars, in order to be accredited, in order for students to transfer, in order to get students to come, colleges have felt the necessity to be like everyone else. Management is too complex to simply blame the president or the dean. They, like other managers in higher education, tend to be a part of the system and cannot be expected to stand against it.

In spite of recent efforts to include students in the governance of private institutions, they in no way can be charged with a share of poor management. Their voices, while heard in growing numbers, have never dominated any segment of management beyond student government, which has rarely affected the life of any institution of higher learning. Some managers have acted out of a concern for what students want or need, but students cannot be credited with any significant part of the management of the institutions examined in this book.

The results of poor management for these colleges have been too many faculty hired, too many courses taught, too many majors designed, too many small classes meeting, and too many administrators overseeing the program. In contrast, there have been too few students enrolled, too few dollars generated, and too little credit-hour productivity from faculty. The tendency to spend money before it is in hand, to expand programs on the basis of promise rather than product, and to teach everything that is known in order to be excellent has gone unchallenged in too many institutions for two decades.

Effectiveness as a Purpose

Private higher education now has a chance to develop another purpose in addition to growth, distinctiveness, and excellence. This additional purpose—effectiveness—has its primary focus in good economics. Being effective does not imply efficiency experts, institutional researchers as presidents, or bureaucrats without brains. Effectiveness can be a legitimate purpose of any college. Effectiveness can be the key to a distinctive program, to an excellent program, and to an efficient program.

Effectiveness as an institutional purpose implies accountability and evaluation. It certainly is distinctive. But most of all, effectiveness suggests good management: management that places more emphasis on the product than on the process of education, that understands the distinction between means and ends, that has full control of most of the variables that shape a college. Effective management ranges from students through boards of trustees and outside agencies who apply skills and insights previously not common in postsecondary education. Effectiveness is achieved by management that sees all aspects of a college as parts of an interrelated whole. Although poor management is not alone to blame for the situation of the private college, good management can go a long way toward correcting the problems.

Effectiveness requires a new management style that has at least four characteristics not always common in past management of institutions of higher education.

Private higher education needs trained managers who will solve problems rather than imitate models. In an agrarian society modeling is an appropriate mechanism for introducing change as well as maintaining stability in the culture. Families, churches, schools, governments, and armies in the American society have been based upon models of earlier behavior as the primary mechanism for preservation. But in a technological society in which change occurs very rapidly, modeling moves too slowly—at the rate of generations of people—to maintain stability for that culture.

Very little attention has been given in education to the development of problem-solving skills that industries long ago recognized as necessary for their preservation. Critical thinking, planning, and analysis—along with the ability to make wise judgments in choosing alternatives—are central skills in problem solving. These skills are rarely taught as a central focus of any curriculum from primary through tertiary education. They are the management skills deeply needed by private higher education if it is to maintain its competitive place in the American system of postsecondary education.

Private higher education needs trained managers who can challenge assumptions of higher education. Nearly every practice in private higher education examined in this report could be accomplished less expensively if certain assumptions were challenged—assumptions about ways of organizing learning, ways of teaching students, and the most appropriate aspects of a program to be evaluated. Innovation, for example, has been expensive in small colleges because they have tended to imitate the university; that is, their innovative programs are simply duplications. The secret to more effective and less expensive innovation is to challenge the assumption on which present programs or new programs are based. Several examples present themselves from recent studies in the literature of higher education:

1. *Assumption:* Ph.D.s are preferred faculty. *Challenge:* Ph.D.s most certainly cost more than M.A.s or B.A.s, but there is no evidence that collectively they produce more learning.
2. *Assumption:* All college teachers need subject degrees. *Challenge:* Not all learning is subject oriented. Skills and attitudes may even be more important than cognitive knowledge in liberal arts education.
3. *Assumption:* All college teachers need college degrees. *Challenge:* Is a baccalaureate or a master's degree the most appropriate way by which artists and writers are prepared? A growing body of research suggests that peer teaching can be more effective than teaching by traditionally prepared faculty, particularly at the beginning level of study. Upper-division students can teach freshman composition, handle laboratories, direct tutorials, tutor, teach underprepared students, advise, and carry out a variety of other tasks traditionally assigned to highly paid and prepared faculty.

4. *Assumption:* Libraries should focus on books in a central location, with several professional staff on duty at all times. *Challenge:* Increasingly, the emphasis in libraries is upon information retrieval. The use of paraprofessionals in mini-libraries scattered around the campus, with several general collections where students live and study, may be a more appropriate concept and would not require a central staff or facility.

5. *Assumption:* Colleges should provide food services, athletic programs, and central student unions. *Challenge:* Colleges of the rest of the world do not provide these services; why do American colleges think they must?

6. *Assumption:* The liberal arts is a body of information; therefore, a liberal arts college must teach a body of information in a traditional way. *Challenge:* Since very little is known about the effect of teaching a distribution of subjects, why not conceive of the liberal arts as a way of learning any body of information or skills that produce an independent learner?

7. *Assumption:* Every graduate must have a major in the college from which he is graduated. *Challenge:* Consortia have helped overcome this assumption. Increasingly, students are being graduated from institutions where they did not receive their major. Some institutions give credit for evaluation of life experiences and are willing to acknowledge a major developed in an apprenticeship, from a proprietary school, from a community college, or from any number of other sources separate from an accredited liberal arts college—leaving the liberal arts institution free to provide a basic general education leading to a baccalaureate degree.

8. *Assumption:* Every college needs a business manager, a purchasing agent, a dean of students, a personal counselor, an infirmary, and many other services. *Challenge:* Such services might best be accomplished in concert with other colleges or other community agencies at much less cost.

9. *Assumption:* Small classes produce better learning. *Challenge:* Although most faculty acknowledge that there is very little research evidence to support such a conclusion, they still insist that small classes are a reflection of the purposes of a small college. What little evidence there is about class size suggests that classes can be too small more damagingly than they can be too large.

Private higher education needs trained managers who can apply change strategies. Numerous well-established strategies for change in higher education have enabled effective managers to help people initiate, handle, and implement changes in organization, program, and methodology: holding workshops and retreats, orienting new faculty, trying pilot programs, reorganizing campus government, bringing in experts, and joining consortia. A number of newer strategies also have been developed: problem-solving training sessions, surveys of faculty and students, open hearings on controversial issues, ad hoc organization of task forces to accomplish particular activities, establishment of an educational development officer, visits to other campuses whose activities might serve as models, and the creation of change-agent teams within an institution. Whatever the strategies, managers in private higher education need to know the ways by which people can change without excessive stress and without sabotaging programs to which they have given intellectual assent. Using change strategies is a technique that can help people invest more of themselves in institutions and thus become more committed to meet changing needs as they arise.

Perhaps the most critical part of understanding and applying change strategies is to develop throughout an institution an attitude of self-renewal—the ability of institutions to renew themselves. Static colleges, those in which change is disruptive and difficult, do not understand or apply effective change strategies. Faculty talk about the old curriculum and the new curriculum. Administrators heave a sigh of relief when the self-study is completed because it will not have to be done for another ten years. Long-range planning, if it is done at all, is annually checked off; administrators examine the extent to which they did or did not meet their goals, but no revision of the plan is made semiannually or annually, nor is the plan constantly being changed. In static institutions the faculty vote to limit new ideas. Curriculum committees and administrators respond to ideas from lower in the bureaucracy but rarely initiate new ideas. Evaluation, self-study, and analysis are not dominant characteristics of a static institution. In contrast, a dynamic, self-renewing college is continually examining itself, continually looking for more effective ways to meet its objectives, continually challenging the assumptions on which its program is based, continually gathering data about itself. Managers of liberal arts colleges need to develop the skills that will enable them to lead their institutions toward self-renewal.

Private higher education needs trained managers who can evaluate thoroughly. Evaluation helps to eliminate the inefficient and promote the most effective. In other words, evaluation helps a manager discover optimum ratios and relationships, optimum productivity for minimum cost, maximum output for minimum input. Evaluation enhances the respect that foundations, government, parents, students, and the general public have for an institution. Institutions that are accountable for every dollar they spend and every resource they utilize, that can document the extent to which they have changed students or produced graduates who compete successfully in whatever arena they have chosen, will have the ear of the public and the hand of investors in higher education. Virtually no institution today can say much about the rate of learning of its graduates or the quality of graduates produced. Comparative evaluations certainly aid institutions in this task, and internal evaluations establish baselines for change and for challenging assumptions about traditional ways of teaching and learning.

Recommendations

There are a number of practical ways of applying these four management skills to the problems presented in this book. A dozen specific suggestions are made here from among many alternatives. These recommendations relate entirely to the earlier analyses of curricula and related activities. Each of the practical suggestions outlined is designed to reduce costs, to increase efficiency, and to increase effectiveness if possible without impairing the effectiveness of programs now offered in these liberal arts colleges.

1. *Maintain a 1-to-5 ratio between part-time and full-time faculty and staff.* The 20 percent figure is arbitrary. Any percentage lower than that is not likely to be enough to handle changes that may occur within a single year in an institution. A ratio higher than 1 to 5 may jeopardize the advising and committee functions of the institution, placing too much burden on fewer full-time people to carry out these tasks. Accrediting associations have not responded favorably to a high percentage of part-time people, partly because of the traditional ways in which higher education has gone about its

business, but partly out of ignorance—the questionable assumption that full-time people produce better-quality graduates than part-time people.

As faculty members retire, regardless of the importance of their field to the life of the institution, they could be replaced with part-time people until the 20 percent figure is approximated. Likewise for administrative staff. Faculty and staff positions can be mixed to a greater extent than ego in the past has permitted. A number of faculty can successfully carry out second- and third-level administrative responsibilities and teach part-time as a way of increasing institutional flexibility.

2. *Hire faculty with flexible skills.* Historically, persons employed in liberal arts colleges frequently were able to teach a number of subjects. In this century, with the pressure to specialize and the rewards for research and publication, faculty increasingly have been able to do fewer and fewer different things. The economic press that private colleges are experiencing may force faculty members to teach in at least two if not three or four different fields. Those persons who can do so are easily juggled within a curriculum, are better risks for tenure, and will contribute to the stability of an institution. Morale is maintained and intellectualism is supported by master faculty who can move freely from discipline to discipline, thus not requiring an institution to cut people because of dollar shortages. As faculty members retire, other flexible faculty can fill these gaps by teaching less of one thing and more of another. The continuity of the institution is maintained along with the morale.

3. *Develop a strong institutional research office.* An institutional research office, designed as an adjunct of the president's office, should undertake an immediate and thorough market analysis of student potential, dollar potential, program potential, and product-utilization potential. Studies of prospective students, attrition rates and the dropouts themselves, number of persons going into graduate school, potential job market, potential new fields needed, new careers available, dollar resources available—all need to be known immediately by decision makers in small colleges. These are the particular pieces of information they have lacked. When coupled with the kinds of data available in this study, these pieces of information will enable managers to make more effective qualitative judg-

ments about the future of their institutions and provide the basis for
effective planning.

4. *Develop long-range plans.* A whole chapter (Chapter
Seven) has been devoted to this concept. Very little more needs to
be said except to reiterate and reinforce the need as the paramount
manifestation of effective management.

5. *Participate in cooperative efforts with other institutions.*
Consortia are beginning to realize some of the economic gains that
can be made from cooperative activity, but real economic gain has
yet to be seen, partially because cooperative arrangements have been
quite small and partially because economy has not been an aim of
most arrangements. When twenty to forty institutions come together
for a single purpose, they are able to get discounts for the purchasing
office, buy books and supplies, use computers, increase library pur-
chases, and improve audits for considerably less money than individual institutions are able to command. Insurance, auditing,
computer service, library book processing and purchasing are but a
few of the services that institutions collectively can buy more cheaply.
If some assumptions could be challenged, institutions collectively
might well purchase more central management skills. They might,
for instance, operate one business office for a number of institutions
or develop specialized majors not offered in other colleges.

6. *Reduce the size of the faculty and the administration.*
This is a temporary solution which colleges can utilize once or twice,
but there must be a minimum below which effective learning cannot
be produced. Although the colleges in this project saved about one
million dollars by reducing faculty and administrators, that figure
reflects only 7 percent of their combined deficit and only 1 percent
of their total educational and general expenditure. One million dollars
is nowhere near an adequate saving for them; and if they continue
to cut as they have been doing, their program may be damaged. On
the other hand, most private colleges have more faculty and administrators than they need to produce the present quality of graduates. As
the study of three pairs of institutions in Chapter Five amply demonstrates, at least half of those colleges had far too many faculty. This
figure can be extrapolated for all of private higher education and
still be a conservative reflection of the number of people needed to
carry out present purposes.

7. *Develop plans and programs for reducing attrition.* As Binning (1971, pp. 174–175) has pointed out, "A student with the ability to pay represents $2914 annually to the average private college when tuition, fees, room, board, and the cost of student recruiting are totaled. The average private college dismissed or suspended for academic reasons forty students during academic year 1969–70. Looked at another way, the average private college flunked out nearly $120,000—about the size of the average private college deficit."

Colleges can reduce attrition by designing better advising and orientation programs and more effective freshman-year curricula, by listening more meaningfully to what students say about their education, and by carefully studying student factors that correlate with persistence in or withdrawal from a given institution. Astin's (1972) study of college dropouts is the only current substantive national statement than can serve as a guideline for colleges which wish to examine their own attrition rates and causes.

8. *Increase enrollment.* As demonstrated earlier, increasing enrollment is not necessarily a solution to the problem of the small college unless the number of faculty and number of courses can be held constant. If enrollment is increased without adding faculty or courses to the curriculum, the result is larger classes and greater faculty productivity, measured in student credit hours. When enrollment and faculty production increase, faculty must teach additional students in many classes. Although they may not have more preparations, they do have to read more student papers, hear more student reports, counsel and advise more students, and thus expend more of their energy. Faculty in private colleges work hard, averaging about sixty hours a week (Bowen and Douglas, 1972b, pp. 24–25). They appear to be willing to undertake this additional work, as they often have in the past, to help private higher education sustain itself. There is, however, no point in increasing enrollment if faculty or staff is also increased. No economic gains can be made.

9. *Expect administrators to teach.* Just as faculty with flexible skills should be sought, administrators also need to be able to do more than one thing. Each administrator of a private college could teach one course a year, or two courses a year in institutions that have January terms. This would provide a great deal more flexibility

in faculty hiring and, theoretically at least, relieve the need for one or two full-time-equivalent faculty (based on the number of administrators in even the smallest college). Since most administrators were formerly faculty members, they usually have a discipline field and can teach something to undergraduates. Even if they are specialists in higher education, there are courses in higher education and in college life which they can handle effectively. They should know something about social science research techniques, statistics, or related subjects which, though not always aligned in traditional ways, might provide sound interdisciplinary study for advanced students.

There seems to be no sound argument against administrators teaching except that they are too busy. People make work to fill their days. If priority is given to teaching and every administrator when hired is expected to teach, other tasks which administrators normally do might be dropped or assigned to students or to less expensive paraprofessionals.

10. *Relate budget spending to income.* As Virginia Smith (1972, p. 39) points out, "Budget processes of many institutions divorce responsibility for securing revenue from responsibilities for spending." Unlike almost any other social institution, with the possible exception of orchestras and hospitals, colleges do not give the persons responsible for collecting funds full responsibility for spending them, and those persons who do spend the funds have little responsibility for collecting them. This basic economic conflict presents some serious problems for both faculty and administrators. Such problems can best be overcome by establishing guidelines for income and expenditure. Income guidelines can determine acceptable income sources such as percentage distribution of income (particularly the percent which should come from student fees) and the kinds of research an institution will accept, focusing particularly on research that relates to the main purposes of liberal education and does not divert energies and dollars that later must be assumed by the college. Expenditure guidelines should outline percentage distribution for all educational and general expenditures. This distribution would determine how any additional funds or any losses of funds would be divided among the various activities of the institution.

Some colleges have guidelines by which funds not spent by

April 1 for supplies, equipment, and materials are forefeited. Other institutions require all salary increases to be contingent upon enrollment. A variety of other expenditure policies can be determined. Once guidelines are established, then spending proceeds more easily without the sense of threat, empire building, or stock piling that can pervade institutions without guidelines.

11. *Change concepts of purchasing.* Traditionally, institutions prepare budgets and order new materials and equipment in late spring or early summer for delivery before school starts. Dollars are committed far ahead of enrollments—a procedure that generates at least a cash-flow problem if not a genuine deficit in case students do not materialize. Colleges could change their purchasing patterns by challenging the assumption that new materials need to be available at the beginning of the year. If new materials were made available at the beginning of the second semester of each year, then the pattern would remain constant but be moved forward four months. By this means colleges could place their orders after students are enrolled or shortly before they do enroll, with cancelation privileges well before delivery date. This kind of purchasing, while not affecting large amounts of money, is at least a meaningful way of dealing with some 5 to 10 percent of most college budgets when charges for all departments, administrative offices, and plant maintenance are combined.

12. *Develop economic policy guidelines for the curriculum.* Number of courses, number of majors, and size of classes are the three most critical areas needing overall guidelines. When these are established by the faculty and administration in concert, the curriculum is easier to review and an economic balance is easier to maintain.

Earlier in this study, small colleges were urged to offer no more than six to twelve hours beyond the number required for the major in any academic year. Bowen and Douglass (1972) recommend no more than eleven different courses per year in a subject, or 225 different courses for a total institution. Bowen (1972b, pp. 33–34) points out, "On the testimony of experienced and capable teachers, the number of courses offered in a typical undergraduate college could be halved without harming educational quality." Either of these guidelines could be utilized by private colleges. In addition, some institutions specify that no new courses may be added to the curriculum unless one other course is dropped or combined with an existing course.

A college should offer no more than one major for every three full-time-equivalent faculty members. Such a procedure allows persons to be free to teach in the major and, at the same time, to provide the service and general education courses necessary for the total institution. A major, to continue, must graduate at least five persons a year, determined by averaging the number of graduates in the past two years with the number presently enrolled in the final two years of a program. This policy has been adopted by a number of institutions struggling with the decision about which majors to sustain and which to eliminate.

The Academy for Educational Development (1972, p. 2) recommends a student-faculty ratio of approximately 19 or 20 to 1, which is in line with legislation in Arizona, Kansas, Montana, New Mexico, Missouri, and Minnesota. In New York, Ohio, California, and a number of other states, pending bills will establish specific requirements in public institutions for the ratio of students to faculty. If public institutions can produce a reasonably qualified graduate at the ratio of 20 to 1, there is no reason to believe that private institutions cannot do as well.

Class-size guidelines established by a number of colleges state that courses enrolling fewer than ten students may not be taught unless the course is required for graduation by currently enrolled seniors or unless it is an independent study. Although the elimination of courses after faculty load has been set for a term does not help in that term, it does help institutions plan and project future offerings; and it helps faculty members join in the recruitment of students for their courses, particularly if they are electives. Another way of reducing small classes and number of courses is to offer courses only in alternate years. Many institutions require such alternate-year offerings for all electives that enroll fewer than ten students.

These practical ways of applying management skills to the problems of private higher education will not ensure the survival of these institutions. On the other hand, some of the institutions that participated in this study and have begun to utilize some of the suggestions made here seem to be on the road to recovery and should be around for a long time. Many private colleges evidently still have time to redeem themselves, provided they can muster all their energies in more than temporary activity. Most of the above-named suggestions are only temporary solutions to longer-range problems, which attitudes of self-renewal, trained management skills, and careful long-range planning can correct. Cost effectiveness is only the first of many steps.

ㅋㅋㅋㅋㅋㅋ

General Bibliography

Academy for Educational Development. *Fewer Teachers for More Money.* New York: Academy for Educational Development, 1972.

AIGNER, D. J., AND CHU, S. F. "On Estimating the Industry Production Function." *American Economic Review,* Sept. 1968, *58,* 826–837.

ALIOTO, R. F., AND JUNGHERR, J. *Operational PPBS for Education. A Practical Approach to Effective Decision-Making.* New York: Harper and Row, 1971.

American Council on Education. *College and University Business Administration.* (Rev. Ed.) Washington, D.C., 1968.

An Analysis of Institutional Expenditures for Institutions of Higher Education in the Northeast United States. Buffalo: State University of New York at Buffalo, 1970.

ASTIN, A. W. "Undergraduate Achievement and Institutional Excellence." *Science,* Aug. 1968, *161,* 661–668.

ASTIN, A. W. *Predicting Academic Performance in College: Selective Data for 2,300 American Colleges.* New York: Free Press, 1971.

ASTIN, A. W. *College Dropouts: A National Profile.* Washington, D.C.: American Council on Education, 1972.

ASTIN, A., AND LEE, C. B. *The Invisible Colleges.* New York: McGraw-Hill, 1972.

BAIN, J. S. "Economies of Scale, Concentration, and Condition of Entry in Twenty Manufacturing Industries." *American Economic Review,* 1954, *44,* 15–39.

BALDERSTON, F. E. "Thinking About the Outputs of Higher Education." Paper P–5. Berkeley: Ford Foundation Program for Research in University Administration, University of California, 1970.

BALDERSTON, F. E. *Cost Analysis in Higher Education.* Berkeley: Ford Foundation Program for Research in University Administration, University of California, 1972a.

BALDERSTON, F. E. *Varieties of Financial Crisis.* Berkeley: Ford Foundation Program for Research in University Administration, University of California, 1972b.

BAUMOL, W. "Macroeconomics of Unbalanced Growth: The Anatomy of Urban Crisis." *American Economic Review,* June 1967, *42,* 415–426.

BAUMOL, W., AND BOWEN, W. G. "On the Performing Arts: The Anatomy of their Economic Problems." *American Economic Review,* May 1965, *55,* 495–502.

BELL, C. "Can Mathematical Models Contribute to Efficiency in

Higher Education?" In Carnegie Commission on Higher Education, *Papers on Efficiency in the Management of Higher Education.* New York: McGraw-Hill, 1972.

BERELSON, B. *Graduate Education in the United States.* New York: McGraw-Hill, 1960.

BINNING, D. W. "Admissions: A Key to Financial Stability." *Liberal Education,* 1971, *57* (2), 173–180.

BLAUG, M. *Economics of Education.* New York: Penguin Books, 1969.

BOGARD, L. "Management in Institutions of Higher Education. In *Papers on Efficiency in the Management of Higher Education.* New York: McGraw-Hill, 1972.

BOLIN, J. G., AND MC MURRAIN, T. *Student-Faculty Ratios in Higher Education.* Athens: Institute of Higher Education, University of Georgia, 1969.

BOTTOMLEY, J. A. *Cost-Effectiveness in Higher Education.* Bradford, Yorkshire, England: Bradford University, 1971. ED 054 749.

BOWEN, H. R. "Can Higher Education Become More Efficient?" *Educational Record,* 1972a, *53* (3), 191–200.

BOWEN, H. R. "Effective Education at Reasonable Costs." In W. Godwin (Ed.), *Higher Education: Myths, Realities and Possibilities.* Atlanta, Ga.: Southern Regional Educational Board, 1972b.

BOWEN, H. R., AND DOUGLASS, G. K. "Cutting Instructional Costs." In W. Jellema (Ed.), *Efficient College Management.* San Francisco: Jossey-Bass, 1972a.

BOWEN, H. R., AND DOUGLASS, G. K. *Efficiency in Liberal Education.* New York: McGraw-Hill, 1972b.

BOWEN, W. G. *The Economics of the Major Private Universities.* New York: McGraw-Hill, 1968.

BOWLES, S. "Towards an Educational Production Function." In W. L. Hansen (Ed.), *Education Income and Human Capital*. New York: Columbia University Press, 1970.

BOYER, E. L. *The Impact of Institutional Research on the Academic Program*. Albany: Office of the Vice Chancellor for University-Wide Activities, State University of New York, 1969.

BRANDL, J. E. "Public Service Outputs of Higher Education: An Exploratory Essay." In *Outputs of Higher Education*. Boulder, Colo.: Western Interstate Commission on Higher Education, July 1970.

BRENEMAN, D. W. "The Stability of Faculty Input Coefficients in Linear Workload Models of the University of California." Paper 69–4. Berkeley: Ford Foundation Program for Research in University Administration, University of California, 1969.

BRENEMAN, D. W. "The Ph.D. Production Function: The Case at Berkeley." Paper P–16. Berkeley: Ford Foundation Program for Research in University Administration, University of California, 1970.

BRENEMAN, D. W. "Internal Pricing Within the University—A Conference Report." Paper P–24. Berkeley: Ford Foundation Program for Research in University Administration, University of California, 1971.

BRENEMAN, D. W., AND WEATHERSBY, G. B. "Definition and Measurement of the Activities and Outputs of Higher Education." Discussion paper 10. Berkeley: Ford Foundation Program for Research in University Administration, University of California, 1970.

BROWN, D. B. "A Scheme for Measuring the Output of Higher Education." In *Outputs of Higher Education*. Boulder, Colo.: Western Interstate Commission on Higher Education, July 1970.

BROWN, R. N. "Instructional Systems Development: Cost and Content in College Courses." *Educational Technology*, 1971, *11*, 26–27.

BRUMBAUGH, A. J. *Issues of Implementing Institutional Research*. Atlanta, Ga.: Southern Regional Education Board, 1968.

BUSHNELL, D. D., AND ALLEN, D. W. *The Computer in American Education.* New York: Wiley, 1967.

CAIN, G. G., AND WATTS, H. W. "Problems in Making Policy Inferences from the Coleman Report." *American Sociological Review,* Apr. 1970, *35,* 228–243.

California Coordinating Council for Higher Education. *Higher Cost Programs in California Public Higher Education.* Report 71–3. Mar. 1971.

CALLAHAN, R. *Education and the Cult of Efficiency.* Chicago: University of Chicago Press, 1962.

Carnegie Commission on Higher Education. *New Students, New Places.* New York: McGraw-Hill, 1971.

Carnegie Commission on Higher Education. *Institutional Aid: Federal Support to Colleges and Universities.* New York: McGraw-Hill, 1972a.

Carnegie Commission on Higher Education. *The More Effective Use of Resources: An Imperative for Higher Education.* New York: McGraw-Hill, 1972b.

CARTER, C. F. "The Efficiency of Universities." *Higher Education,* Feb. 1972, 77–90.

CARTTER, A. *An Assessment of Quality in Graduate Education.* Washington, D.C.: American Council on Education, 1966.

CASASCO, J. A. *Corporate Planning Models for University Management.* Report 4. Washington, D.C.: ERIC Clearinghouse on Higher Education, 1970.

CAVANAUGH, A. D. *A Preliminary Evaluation of Cost Studies in Higher Education.* Berkeley: Office of Institutional Research, University of California, 1969.

CHASE, H. C. *Cost Analysis in Higher Education: A Review with*

Recommendations for Allied Health Educational Program. Washington, D.C.: Association of Schools of Allied Health Professions, 1970.

CHEIT, E. F. *The New Depression in Higher Education: A Study of Financial Conditions at 41 Colleges and Universities*. New York: McGraw-Hill, 1971.

CHUANG, Y. C. *An Educational Planning System: Cost-Effectiveness Approach*. 1972. ED 061 644.

A Conceptual Framework for Institutional Research. Proceedings of the Fourth Annual Forum of the Association for Institutional Research. Athens, Ga., 1964.

COOMBS, P. H., AND HALLAK, J. *Managing Education Costs*. New York: Oxford University Press, 1972.

Cost Study Manual 1965–66. Springfield: Illinois State Board of Higher Education, 1966.

CREAGER, J. "Futurism and Higher Education." *Change*, 1972, *4*, 62–63.

DANO, S. *Industrial Production Models*. New York: Springer-Verlag, 1966.

DIEWERT, W. E. "Functional Form in the Theory of Production and Consumer Demand." Unpublished doctoral dissertation. Berkeley: University of California, 1968.

DIEWERT, W. E. "An Application of the Shephard Duality Theorem: A Generalized Leontief Production Function." *Journal of Political Economy*, May–June 1971, *79*, 481–507.

DRESSEL, P. L. "A Comprehensive and Continuing Program of Institutional Research." In E. J. McGrath and L. R. Meeth (Eds.), *Cooperative Long-Range Planning in Liberal Arts Colleges*. New York: Teachers College Press, 1964.

DRESSEL, P. L. *Institutional Research in the University: A Handbook*. San Francisco: Jossey-Bass, 1971.

DRUCKER, P. "What Principles of Management Can the President of a Small College Use to Improve the Efficiency of His Organization?" In E. McGrath (Ed.), *Selected Issues in College Administration*. New York: Teachers College Press, 1967.

EADS, G., NERLOVE, M., AND RADUCHEL, W. "A Long-Run Cost Function for the Local Service Airline Industry: An Experiment in Non-Linear Estimation." *Review of Economics and Statistics*, Aug. 1969, 258–270.

EMERSON, H. *Twelve Principles of Efficiency*. New York: Engineering Magazine Co., 1913.

FARRAR, D., AND GLAUBER, R. "Multicollinearity in Regression Analysis: The Problem Revisited." *Review of Economics and Statistics*. Feb. 1967, 92–107.

FARRELL, M. J. "The Measurement of Productive Efficiency." *Journal of the Royal Statistical Society*, Series A, Part III, 1957, *120*, 253–290.

FARRELL, M. J., AND FIELDHOUS, M. "Estimating Efficient Production Functions Under Increasing Returns to Scale." *Journal of the Royal Statistical Society*, Series A, Part II, 1962, *125*, 252–267.

FEINSTEIN, O. *Higher Education in the United States—Economics, Personalism, Quality*. Lexington, Mass.: Lexington Books, 1971.

FELDSTEIN, M. S. *Economic Analysis for Health Service Efficiency*. Chicago: Markham, 1968.

FINCHER, C. (Ed.) *Institutional Research and Academic Outcomes*. Athens, Ga.: Association for Institutional Research, 1968.

Five College Cooperation: Directions for the Future. Report of the Five College Long-Range Planning Committee. Amherst, Mass.: University of Massachusetts Press, 1969.

GEOFFRION, A. M., DYER, J. S., AND FEINBERG, A. "Academic Departmental Management: An Application of an Interactive Multi-Criterion Optimization Approach." Paper P–25. Berkeley: Ford Foundation Program for Research in University Administration, University of California, 1971.

GROSS, E., AND GRAMBSCH, P. *Academic Administrators and University Goals.* Washington, D.C.: American Council on Education, 1968.

GULKO, W. W. *Program Classification Structure—Preliminary Edition for Review.* Boulder, Colo.: Western Interstate Commission on Higher Education, 1970.

GULKO, W. W. "Unit Costs of Instruction: A Methodological Approach." In *Cost Finding Principles and Procedures.* Boulder, Colo.: Western Interstate Commission on Higher Education, 1971.

HALLAK, J. *The Analysis of Educational Costs and Expenditure.* New York: International Institute for Educational Planning, UNESCO, 1969.

HANOCH, G. "Homotheticity in Joint Productions." *Journal of Economic Theory,* Dec. 1970, *2,* 423–426.

HANOCH, G., AND ROTHSCHILD, M. "Testing the Assumptions of Production Theory—A Nonparametric Approach." *Journal of Political Economy,* Mar–Apr. 1972, *80,* 256–275.

HANSEN, W. L., AND WEISBROD, B. A. *Benefits, Costs, and Finance of Public Higher Education.* Chicago: Markham, 1969.

HANSEN, W. L., KELLEY, A. C., AND WEISBROD, B. A. "Economic Efficiency and the Distribution of Benefits from College Instruction." *American Economic Review,* May 1970, *60,* 364–369.

HARRIS, S. *Higher Education: Resources and Finance.* New York: McGraw-Hill, 1962.

HARTLEY, H. J. *Educational Planning-Programming-Budgeting: A Systems Approach.* Englewood Cliffs, N.J.: Prentice-Hall, 1968.

HENDERSON, J., AND QUANDT, R. *Microeconomic Theory: A Mathematical Approach.* New York: McGraw-Hill, 1958.

HOUGH, R. "The Outputs of Undergraduate Education." In *Outputs of Higher Education*. Boulder, Colo.: Western Interstate Commission on Higher Education, July 1970, 93–104.

HUNGATE, T. L., AND MEETH, L. R. "The Quality and Cost of Liberal Arts College Programs." In E. J. McGrath and L. R. Meeth (Eds.), *Cooperative Long Range Planning in Liberal Arts Colleges*. New York: Teachers College Press, Columbia University, 1964.

IKENBERRY, S. O. "Instructional Cost and Quality." *College and University*, 1962, *37* (3), 242–250.

IKENBERRY, S. O. "Institutional Research and the Instructional Process." In G. Drewry (Ed.), *The Instructional Process and Institutional Research*. Athens, Ga.: Association for Institutional Research, 1967.

JELLEMA, W. "The Red and the Black: A Preview." *Liberal Education*, 1971a, *57*, 147–159.

JELLEMA, W. *Redder and Much Redder*. Washington, D.C.: Association of American Colleges, 1971b.

JELLEMA, W. *Efficient College Management*. San Francisco: Jossey-Bass, 1972.

JELLEMA, W. *From Red to Black?* San Francisco: Jossey-Bass, 1973.

JENKINS, W., AND LEHMAN, G. "Nine Pitfalls of PPBS." *School Management*, 1972, *16* (2).

JENNY, H., AND WYNN, G. *The Golden Years*. Wooster, Ohio: College of Wooster, 1970.

JENNY, H., AND WYNN, G. *The Turning Point*. Wooster, Ohio: College of Wooster, 1972.

JOHNSON, C. B., AND KATZENMEYER, W. G. (Eds.), *Management Information Systems in Higher Education: The State of the Art*. Durham, N.C.: Duke University Press, 1969.

184   L. Richard Meeth

JOHNSON, D. L. "Admissions: The Key to Fiscal Stability." *Liberal Education,* 1971, *57* (2).

JUSTER, F. "Microdata Requirements and Public Policy Designs." *Annals of Economic and Social Measurement,* Jan. 1972.

KEENE, T. "Use-Efficiency Model for Planning Instructional Space Requirements." *College and University,* 1972, *47,* 176–183.

KEENE, T. W. *Instructional Program Costs at the University of South Florida Division of Planning and Analysis.* Tampa: University of South Florida, 1968.

KELLER, J. F. "Higher Education Objectives: Measures of Performance and Effectiveness." Paper P–7. Berkeley: Ford Foundation Program for Research in University Administration, University of California, 1970.

KERSHAW, J. A., AND MOOD, A. M. "Resource Allocation in Higher Education." *American Economic Review,* May 1970, *60,* 341–346.

KNORR, O. A. (Ed.) *Long-Range Planning in Higher Education.* Boulder, Colo.: Western Interstate Commission for Higher Education, 1965.

KRAFT, R. H. P., AND LATTA, R. F. "Systems Approach in Educational Planning and Management." *Educational Technology,* Feb. 1972, 5–79.

LAU, L. J., AND YOTOPOULOS, P. A. "A Test for Relative Efficiency and Application to Indian Agriculture." *American Economic Review,* Mar. 1971, *61,* 94–109.

LAVE, J. R., AND LAVE, L. B. "Hospital Cost Functions." *American Economic Review,* June 1970, *60,* 379–395.

LAWRENCE, B. "The Western Interstate Commission for Higher Education Information Systems Program." In C. B. Johnson and W. G. Katzenmeyer (Eds.), *Management Information Systems in Higher Education, the State of the Art.* Durham, N.C.: Duke University Press, 1969.

LAWRENCE, B., AND JONES, D. *The Cooperative Development of Planning and Management Systems in Higher Education: The Nature, Scope and Limitations of the WICHE Planning and Management Systems Program.* Boulder, Colo.: Western Interstate Commission for Higher Education, 1971.

LAWRENCE, B., WEATHERSBY, G., AND PATTERSON, V. (Eds.) *Outputs of Higher Education.* Boulder, Colo.: Western Interstate Commission on Higher Education, July 1970.

LAYARD, P. R. G., SARGAN, J. D., AGER, M. E., AND JONES, D. J. *Qualified Manpower and Economic Performance.* London: London School of Economics, Studies on Education, 1972.

LEGGETT, S., AND BINNING, D. "Fourteen Plans in Search of a Place." *College and University Business,* 1971, *50,* 35–42.

LE LONG, D. "Allocating and Utilizing Resources." In P. Dressel (Ed.), *Institutional Research in the University: A Handbook.* San Francisco: Jossey-Bass, 1971.

LEVIN, D. M., AND OTHERS. *A Symposium on Educational Planning and Program Budgeting: An Analysis of Implementation Strategy.* Santa Monica, Calif.: Rand Corporation, 1971.

LEVIN, H. "A Cost-Effectiveness Analysis of Teacher Selection." *Journal of Human Resources,* Winter 1970, *5,* 24–33.

LITTERER, J. *Organizations: Structure and Behavior.* New York: Wiley, 1963.

Long Range Planning: University of Missouri. Columbia: University of Missouri, 1968.

MC GRATH, E. (Ed.) *Prospect for Renewal.* San Francisco: Jossey-Bass, 1972.

MARTIN, W. B. "The Problems of Size." *Journal of Higher Education,* Mar. 1967, *38,* 144–152.

MASON, T. "Fiscal Management and Institutional Priorities:

How Institutional Research Can Help." *Liberal Education,* 1971, *57,* 219–223.

MAYNARD, J. *Some Microeconomics of Higher Education: Economies of Scale.* Lincoln: University of Nebraska, 1971.

MILLER, J. L. "An Introduction to Budgetary Analysis." In E. F. Schietinger (Ed.), *Introductory Papers on Institutional Research.* Atlanta, Ga.: Southern Regional Education Board, 1968.

MOON, R. G. "Beating the High Cost of Low Ratios." In W. Jellema (Ed.), *Efficient College Management.* San Francisco: Jossey-Bass, 1972.

MORISHIMA, J. K. (Ed.) *An Annotated Bibliography of Institutional Research 1970–71.* Berkeley: Office of Institutional Research, University of California, 1971.

MOWBRAY, G., AND LEVINE, J. "Development and Implementation of CAMPUS: A Computer-Based Planning and Budgeting System for Universities and Colleges." *Educational Technology,* 1971, *11,* 27–32.

MUNDLAK, Y. "Empirical Production Function Free of Management Bias." *Journal of Farm Economics,* Feb. 1961, 44–46.

National Center for Educational Statistics. *Financial Characteristics of Institutions of Higher Education.* Washington, D.C.: Government Printing Office, 1970.

NEFF, C. B. "Planning and Governance." *Journal of Higher Education,* 1971, *42,* 116–132.

NERLOVE, M. *Estimation and Identification of Cobb-Douglas Production Functions.* Chicago: Rand McNally, 1965.

NERLOVE, M. "Returns to Scale in Electricity Supply." In A. Zellner (Ed.), *Readings in Economic Statistics and Econometrics.* Boston: Little, Brown, 1968.

NERLOVE, M. "Further Evidence on the Estimation of Dynamic Economic Relations from a Time Series of Cross Sections." *Econometrica,* Mar. 1971, *39,* 359–382.

NEWHOUSE, J. P. "Toward a Theory of Non-Profit Institutions: An Economic Model of a Hospital." *American Economic Review,* Mar. 1970, *60,* 64–74.

NORDELL, L. P. *A Dynamic Input-Output Model of the California Educational System.* Technical report 25. Berkeley: Center for Research in Management Science, University of California, 1967.

Office of the President. "Faculty Effort and Output Study." Report to the Committee on Educational Policy. Berkeley: University of California, Jan. 9, 1970.

O'NEILL, J. *Resource Use in Higher Education: Trends in Outputs and Inputs, 1930 to 1967.* Berkeley: Carnegie Commission on Higher Education, 1971.

PACE, C. R. *Education and Evangelism.* New York: McGraw-Hill, 1972.

PALOLA, E., LEHMAN, T., AND BLISCHKE, W. "The Reluctant Planner: Faculty in Institutional Planning." *Journal of Higher Education,* 1971, *43* (7), 587–602.

PARDEN, R. J. (Ed.) *An Introduction to Program Planning, Budgeting and Evaluation for Colleges and Universities.* Santa Clara: Office of Institutional Planning, University of Santa Clara, 1970.

PARDEN, R. J. "Planning, Programming and Budgeting Systems." *Liberal Education,* 1971, *57,* 202–210.

PERL, L. J. "Graduation, Graduate School Attendance, and Investments in College Training." Paper P–21. Berkeley: Ford Foundation Program for Research in University Administration, University of California, 1971.

PETRIK, E. V. *Planning for Institutional Evolution.* Boulder: University of Colorado, 1967.

PFOUTS, R. "The Theory of Cost of Production in the Multiproduct Firm." *Econometrica,* Oct. 1961, *29,* 650–658.

"Planning-Programming-Budgeting System Reexamined: Development, Analysis, and Criticism." *Public Administration Review,* 1969, *29.*

PLATT, W. J. *Research for Educational Planning: Notes on Emergent Needs.* New York: International Institute for Educational Planning, UNESCO, 1970.

Program Planning-Budgeting-Evaluation System Design: An Annotated Bibliography. Chicago: Research Corporation of the Association of School Business Officials, 1969.

RAMSEY, J., AND ZAREMBKA, P. "Specification Error Tests and Alternative Functional Forms of the Aggregate Production Function." *Journal of the American Statistical Association,* Sept. 1971, *66,* 471.

REICHARD, D. J. *Campus Size: A Selective Review.* Atlanta, Ga.: Southern Regional Education Board, 1971.

ROURKE, F. E., AND BROOKS, G. E. *The Managerial Revolution in Higher Education.* Baltimore: Johns Hopkins Press, 1966.

RUSCOE, G. C. *The Conditions for Success in Educational Planning.* New York: International Institute for Educational Planning, UNESCO, 1969.

RUSSELL, J. "Dollars and Cents: Some Hard Facts." In S. Baskin (Ed.), *Higher Education: Some Newer Developments.* New York: McGraw-Hill, 1963.

SCHIETINGER, E. F. (Ed.) *Introductory Papers on Institutional Research.* Atlanta, Ga.: Southern Regional Education Board, 1968.

SEITZ, W. D. "The Measurement of Efficiency Relative to a Frontier Production Function." *American Journal of Agricultural Economics,* Nov. 1970, 505–511.

SEITZ, W. D. "Productive Efficiency in the Steam-Electric Generating Industry." *Journal of Political Economy,* July–Aug. 1971, *79,* 878–886.

SHUBIK, M. "On Different Methods for Allocating Resources." Paper P–4161. Santa Monica, Calif.: Rand Corporation, 1969.

The Sixty College Study of Income and Expenditures—A Second Look. Washington, D.C.: National Federation of College and University Business Officers Associations, 1957–1958.

SMITH, K. R., MILLER, M., AND GOLLODAY, F. L. "An Analysis of the Optimal Use of Inputs in the Production of Medical Services." Journal of Human Resources, Spring 1972, 7, 208–225.

SMITH, V. B. "More for Less: A New Priority." In O. Mills (Ed.), Universal Higher Education Costs and Benefits. Washington, D.C.: American Council on Education, 1971.

SMITH, V. B. "Assessing and Improving Productivity in Higher Education." In Higher Education: Myths, Realities and Possibilities. Atlanta, Ga.: Southern Regional Education Board, 1972.

SORKIN, A. L. "A Comparison of Quality Characteristics of Negro and White Private and Church Related Colleges and Universities in the South." College and University, 1971, 46 (3), 199–209.

SPLETE, A. P. "The Role of the Academic Planning Office in Innovation." In P. Ritterbush (Ed.), The Bankruptcy of Academic Policy. Washington, D.C.: Acropolis Books, 1972.

"State Expenditure on Higher Education, 1970." Summarized in the Chronicle of Higher Education, October 4 and November 15, 1971.

STECKLEIN, J. E. "Institutional Research." In A. S. Knowles (Ed.), Handbook of College and University Administration. Vol. 1. New York: McGraw-Hill, 1970.

STICKLER, W. H. "The Role of Institutional Research in 'The Managerial Revolution in Higher Education': An Overview." In E. F. Schietinger (Ed.), Introductory Papers on Institutional Research. Atlanta, Ga.: Southern Regional Education Board, 1968.

STIER, W. F. Utilization of the PPBS Concept in the Develop-

ment of a Departmental Budget for a Liberal Arts College. Sioux City, Iowa: Briar Cliff College, 1970.

STUIT, D. "Measuring the Quality of a College or University Environment." In *1961 International Conference on Testing Problems.* Princeton, N.J.: Educational Testing Service, 1961.

SUTTERFIELD, W. "College Planning Could Use HELP." *College and University Business,* 1971, 50, 42–46.

TANNER, C. "Educational Operations Research: An Approach to PPBS Implementation." *Educational Technology,* 1971, *11,* 50–51.

THOMPSON, D. L. "PPBS: The Need for Experience." *Journal of Higher Education,* 1971, *42,* 678–691.

TIMMER, C. P. "Using a Probabilistic Frontier Production Function to Measure Technical Efficiency." *Journal of Political Economy,* July/Aug. 1971, *79,* 776–794.

TOFFLER, A. *Future Shock.* New York: Random House, 1970.

Toward a Long-Range Plan for Federal Financial Support for Higher Education: A Report to the President. Washington, D.C.: Department of Health, Education, and Welfare, 1969.

TYNDALL, D. G., AND BARNES, G. "Unit Costs of Instruction in Higher Education." *Journal of Experimental Education,* 1962, *31,* 114–118.

VAN WIJK, A. P., AND LEVINE, J. *The Pros and Cons of Existing Formula Financing Systems and a Suggested New Approach.* Toronto: Institute for Policy Analysis, University of Toronto, 1969.

VIVEKANANTHAN, P. S. *Development of a Planning System for Educational Research and Development Centers.* Washington, D.C.: National Center for Educational Research and Development, 1971.

WAGNER, W. G., AND WEATHERSBY, G. B. "Optimality in College Planning: A Control Theoretic Approach." Paper P–22. Berkeley: Ford Foundation Program for Research in University Administration, University of California, 1971.

WALTERS, A. A. "Production and Cost Functions: An Econometric Survey." *Econometrica,* Jan./Apr. 1963, *31,* 1–66.

WEATHERSBY, G. B. *The Development of a University Cost Simulation Model.* Berkeley: University of California, 1967.

WEATHERSBY, G. B. "Educational Planning and Decision Making: The Use of Decision and Control Analysis." Paper P–6. Berkeley: Ford Foundation Program for Research in University Administration, University of California, 1970.

WEATHERSBY, G. B. "PPBS; Purpose, Persuasion, Backbone and Spunk." *Liberal Education,* 1971, *57,* 211–218.

WEATHERSBY, G. B., AND WEINSTEIN, M. C. "A Structural Comparison of Analytical Models of University Planning." Paper P–12. Berkeley: Ford Foundation Program for Research in University Administration, University of California, 1970.

WELD, E. A. "Expenditures for Public Institutions of Higher Education, 1969–70." *Journal of Higher Education,* 1972, *43,* 417–440.

Western Interstate Commission on Higher Education. *Objectives and Guidelines of the WICHE Management Information Systems Program.* Boulder, Colo., 1969.

Western Interstate Commission on Higher Education. *Cost Finding Principles and Procedures.* Boulder, Colo., 1971.

Western Interstate Commission on Higher Education. *Faculty Activity Analysis: Overview of Major Issues.* Boulder, Colo., 1971.

WILDAVSKY, A. "Rescuing Policy Analysis from PPBS." *Public Administration Review,* Mar./Apr. 1969, *29,* 189–202.

WING, P., AND BLUMBERG, M. "Operating Expenditures and Sponsored Research at U.S. Medical Schools: An Empirical Study of Cost Patterns." *Journal of Human Resources,* Winter 1971, *6,* 75–102.

WINSLOW, F. D. "The Capital Cost of a University." Paper P–9.

Berkeley: Ford Foundation Program for Research in University Administration, University of California, 1971.

WINSTEAD, P., AND HOBSON, E. "Institutional Goals: Where to from Here?" *Journal of Higher Education,* 1971, *42,* 669–677.

WITMER, D. R. "Cost Studies in Higher Education." *Review of Educational Research,* 1972, *42* (1), 99–127.

WOODHALL, M. *Cost-Benefit Analysis in Educational Planning.* New York: International Institute for Educational Planning, UNESCO, 1970.

ʑʑʑʛʛʛ

Annotated Bibliography

A. Academic Long-Range Planning

BEZDEK, R. H. "Long-Range University Planning in View of an Uncertain Future for College Graduates." *Journal of Higher Education,* 1972, *43,* 267–282. Asserts that long-range planners must accept the responsibilities for assessing the social and vocational opportunities their graduates will face. Develops an empirical methodology whereby the detailed occupational manpower requirements likely to be generated by "alternate economic futures" may be related to demands for college-educated manpower on a regional or statewide basis. Several different concepts of the supply of and demand for educated manpower are discussed, and it is emphasized that the effective demand (backed up by an allocation of resources) is the most important variable to be considered in educational planning. A tight educational budget situation makes it increasingly necessary that those who plan to institute or expand academic programs convince trustees and legislators of a "need" in particular program areas. Projections for the state of Illinois are analyzed. Illustrative statistical tables.

BOLIN, J. G. *Institutional Long-Range Planning.* Athens, Ga.: Institute of Higher Education, University of Georgia, 1969. An excellent, widely used document which comprehensively discusses what must be considered in long-range planning, prepares broad guidelines for evaluating and revising plans, raises many pertinent questions about certain aspects of planning, and probes "internal and external factors" which can cause failure.

CHAMBERS, M. M. *Freedom and Repression in Higher Education.* Bloomington, Ind.: Bloomcraft, 1965. Serious negative note regarding long-range planning; not so much concerned about planning as about the implications for control, which planning threatens.

DRESSEL, P. L., AND DIETRICH, J. E. "Departmental Review and Self-Study." *Journal of Higher Education,* 1967, *38,* 25–37. Gives a ten-point outline, used for departmental self-study at Michigan State University, pertaining to review of departmental philosophy, image, human resources, financial resources, organization and administration, curriculum, basic instructional statistics, physical facilities, liaison with other instructional units, and role within the college and university.

FARMER, J. *An Approach to Planning and Management Systems Implementation.* ED 052 730. 1971. Describes reasons for development and implementation of planning management systems in institutions of higher education; relates the history and significance of the Planning and Management System (PMS) program of the Western Interstate Commission for Higher Education; and compares two approaches to implementation. Six beginning steps are suggested: executive training, development of an analytic capability, implementation of program cost accounting, application of a resource requirement model, application of a student flow model, and selection and implementation of a scheduling model.

FINCHER, C. *Planning in Higher Education.* Athens, Ga.: Institute of Higher Education, University of Georgia, 1966. A concise introduction to the nature of planning, limitations of current methods, criteria for setting priorities, and improvement of planning.

FOX, R. E. *The University of Colorado Guide to Academic Planning.* Boulder: University of Colorado Press, 1967. Describes procedures used in a pilot academic planning program at the University of Colorado. Includes a model of planning functions, a suggested planning calendar, and sample forms used by faculty planning committees.

HARVEY, J. *College and University Planning.* ERIC Clearinghouse on Higher Education, 1971. ED 049 396. Reviews some of the new developments in planning techniques for colleges and universities. Examines the process of planning and two case studies of planning. Special attention is focused on goals and such programing strategies as PPBS and computer-assisted planning.

INMAN, J. C. *Some Principles of Planning for Colleges and Universities.* ED 048 817. 1971. Outlines a systematic approach to long-range planning in colleges and universities. Generally discusses the planning process, then presents seven concrete objectives for planning.

JENKINS, W. A., AND LEHMAN, G. *PPBS Implementation Guidelines.* ED 060 537. 1971. Presents thirty-four guidelines for PPBS. The guidelines (divided into planning, programming, budgeting, and systems analysis) are designed to point out potential trouble spots that could occur at any of the stages of system implementation. This document is based upon current literature, administrative experience, and interaction with PPBS practitioners.

MAYHEW, L. B. "Curriculum Construction and Planning." In Asa S. Knowles (Ed.), *Handbook of College and University Administration.* Vol. 2. New York: McGraw-Hill, 1970. A good overview, with precise definitions of terms (curriculum, course, prerequisites, credit-hour system). Discusses creation of new curricular programs, techniques of curricular study, curricular theory, barriers to curricular construction, techniques and mechanisms for curricular change, long-range curricular budget making, and planning. Emphasis is on the need for long-range planning, forecast for personnel, forecast for financing. See especially pp. 2–52.

MC GRATH, E. J., AND MEETH, L. R. (Eds.) *Cooperative Long-Range Planning in Liberal Arts Colleges.* New York: Teachers College Press, Columbia University, 1964. This relevant document contains articles (by McGrath, Meeth, Thad Hungate, William O'Connell, Paul Dressel, Algo Henderson, and others) which stress the need for continuous and long-term analysis and planning; provide useful procedures for attacking current and prospective academic problems; and present concrete ideas on long-range planning, essential data, appropriate data-collection systems, and viable information exchanges among institutions. Focuses on budgeting, course proliferation, tuition policy, standards of admission, and office of institutional research. See particularly "Continuing Study of the Liberal Arts College"; "The Quality and Cost of Liberal Arts Programs"; "A Comprehensive and Continuing Program of Institutional Research."

MC NAMARA, J. F. "Mathematical Programming Models in Educational Planning." *Review of Educational Research,* 1971, *41,* 419–446. Reviews and assimilates "emerging" literature advocating the use of management science and operation research models as a means to increase the efficiency of academic planning and decisionmaking. Provides a brief overview of mathematical programming: its basic termiology, current applications of mathematical programming techniques to planning problems, future applications in light of recent developments in program planning and budgeting. Stresses need to conduct studies that determine the utility and limitations of management science models.

MEETH, L. R. (Ed.) *Selected Issues in Higher Education: An Annotated Bibliography.* New York: Teachers College Press, Columbia University, 1965. See entry on Long-Range Planning for key references prior to 1965.

MEETH, L. R. "Functional Long-Range Planning: Purpose and Process." *Liberal Education,* 1967, *53,* 375–384. Asserts that involvement in the process of long-range planning is "probably more valuable than the results." Long-range planning is essentially structuring for change, elicits systematic overall direction for an institution, provides the base for institutional continuity, and can best be defined in four steps: (1) forecasting the future in terms of the present—setting institutional goals; (2) ascertaining the needs of that future; (3) ascertaining the resources to fill that need; and (4) making a systematic plan and program to move from the present to the future. Concisely tells how to start a long-range plan.

PETERSON, M. W. "PPBS." *Journal of Higher Education*, 1971, *42*, 1–20. Describes the PPBS process, defining certain basic elements: objectives, program, program alternatives, output, progress measurement, input, systems analysis. The system (PPBS) by which these elements can be related in an academic setting is discussed in three stages: planning, programming, budgeting.

PIELE, P. K. *Planning-Programming-Budgeting Systems*. Educational Management Review Series Number 2. ERIC Clearinghouse on Educational Management, 1972. Surveys documents concerned with the development of PPBS for academic planning, models of PPBS implementation, and bibliographies available on the subject. PPBS decision-making models enable academic managers to identify objectives, delineate programs in order to achieve objectives, analyze alternatives, allocate resources over a period of time, and calculate costs and program effectiveness.

Planning for the 1970's: Higher Education in Colorado. Denver: Colorado Commission on Higher Education, 1971. This statement deals with the possibilities, the planning, and the policies of higher education in Colorado through the 1970s and into the 1980s. The report is designed to assess the needs of institutions in the 1970s; plan for accommodating the upsurge of students; plan for growth with the programs of the institutions; aid the development of higher education in metropolitan areas; review coordination, planning, and governance; and estimate the costs of this expanding program.

THOMPSON, L. M. "Academic Planning." In Asa S. Knowles (Ed.), *Handbook of College and University Administration*. Vol. 1. New York: McGraw-Hill, 1970. A generalized treatment of academic planning: goals and objectives, internal academic organization, policies and regulations, planning academic programs, planning for a new college, planning at an established institution, the analysis of proposals for new or expanded programs.

WILLIAMS, H. *Planning for Effective Resource Allocation in Universities.* Washington, D.C.: American Council on Education, 1966. Stresses the advantages of program-oriented budgeting in universities— allocating resources in accordance with the educational purposes of the institution. Provides useful "sample program budget support sheets" and schedules for budget preparation. Constructs budgetary "review" and decision-making processes (the role of the chief academic officer), discusses problems in establishing a program budgeting system, and makes specific recommendations. Bibliography appended.

B. Institutional Research and Cost Analysis

An Analysis of Instructional Expenditures for Institutions of Higher Education in the Northeast United States. Buffalo: State University of New York at Buffalo, 1970. Identifies common cost patterns as a guideline in determining approach to full utilization of resources; concentrates on 362 institutions stratified by type, control, and the selectivity level of students; educational operating expenses are reviewed in light of changes in the enrollment mix, staffing, and physical plant. One important implication: The productivity of the individual faculty member needs to be increased without increasing class size and capital cost.

BALDERSTON, F. E. *Cost Analysis in Higher Education.* Berkeley: Ford Foundation Program for Research in University Administration, University of California, 1972. Focuses on the uses of cost analysis for institutional management. An excellent overview which covers recent related literature. Bibliography.

BALDERSTON, F. E. *Varieties of Financial Crisis.* Berkeley: Ford Foundation Program for Research in University Administration, 1972. See particularly the section "Cost Trends in Academic Operations."

BOWEN, H. R. "Can Higher Education Become More Efficient?" *Educational Record,* 1972, *53,* 191–200. This economist and college executive explores the elusive meaning of college and university efficiency, and offers some concrete steps by which it may be achieved. States that steady improvements in efficiency cannot be expected to offset all potential cost increases without serious impairment of educational quality, that prospects are good for "slowing down" the rate of increase in cost per student, and that the relationship between expenditure and educational effectiveness is "loose and tenuous." Concludes that the institution that can use fiscal necessity to prune the irrelevant, to find better instructional methods, and to achieve new cooperative relationships with other institutions will emerge in the next decade as a leader. Excellent statistical tables.

BOWEN, H. R., AND DOUGLASS, G. K. *Efficiency in Liberal Education: A Study of Comparative Instructional Costs for Different Ways of Organizing Teaching-Learning in a Liberal Arts College.* New York: McGraw-Hill, 1972. Discusses how a small college (1200 students, 100 faculty) might maintain or improve the quality of education while reducing its cost. To calculate the measurable costs and outputs of instruction at this hypothetical small liberal arts college, six alternative modes of instruction are subjected to special analysis; the authors also examine the effect on cost of changes in faculty teaching load, classroom utilization, proliferation of curricula, distribution of faculty by academic rank, distribution of courses by subject taught, and total college enrollment. Recommendation: that faculty discussions of educational policy be more attuned to budgetary considerations.

BOWEN, H. R., AND DOUGLASS, G. K. "Cutting Instructional Costs." In W. Jellema (Ed.), *Efficient College Management.* San Francisco: Jossey-Bass, 1972. Pp. 79–92. To improve operating efficiency in a liberal arts college, instruction may be organized to reduce cost while maintaining quality.

BOYER, E. L. *The Impact of Institutional Research on the Academic Program.* Albany: Office of the Vice Chancellor for University-Wide Activities, State University of New York, 1969. Constructively examines problems involved in making institutional research effective in the process of academic reform. Reviews current research on subject. An annotated bibliography is appended.

CAVANAUGH, A. D. *A Preliminary Evaluation of Cost Studies in Higher Education.* Berkeley: Office of Institutional Research, University of California, 1969. A succinct yet comprehensive discussion of the strengths and weaknesses of cost analysis in higher education. Annotated bibliography; list of useful state studies and reports.

DRESSEL, P. L., AND OTHERS. *Institutional Research in the University: A Handbook.* San Francisco: Jossey-Bass, 1971. A useful reference book (containing a series of articles by leading practitioners of institutional research) which shows what institutional research actually is, what can be achieved by it, and how it can be established in a particular college or university. Its contents include: major problems in higher education, nature of institutional research in self-study, planning and executing studies, collecting and utilizing basic data, studying environment, studying teaching and learning, evaluating outcomes of instruction, developing and using information systems, allocating and utilizing resources, long-range planning, conducting self-study, wider research, and toward the future.

FINCHER, C. (Ed.) *Institutional Research and Academic Outcomes.* Athens, Ga.: Association for Institutional Research, 1968. Contains a series of excellent articles which discuss a wide range of problems in institutional research, program budgeting, cost analysis, computer application, the roles of management and faculty, long-range planning, management information systems. Models are provided. Bibliographies.

JELLEMA, W. (Ed.) *Efficient College Management.* San Francisco: Jossey-Bass, 1972. A useful book on the fiscal aspects of management in higher education. Fourteen leading writers discuss specific issues and problems involved in program budgeting and institutional research, internal governance and external cooperation, costs of students. Articles focus on managerial purpose and persuasion; planning, programming, and budgeting systems; institutional priorities; institutional research; campus governance and fiscal stability; fiscal implications of collective bargaining; financial aspects of cooperation among institutions; beating the high cost of low ratios; cutting instructional costs; student services; financial status; new approaches to finance; impact of admissions on financial stability; the future of private education.

MILLER, J. L. "An Introduction to Budgetary Analysis." In E. F. Schietinger (Ed.), *Introductory Papers on Institutional Research.* Atlanta, Ga.: Southern Regional Education Board, 1968. A fine introduction to budgetary analysis and decisionmaking. Discusses the purposes of budgetary analysis, historical background, techniques, and patterns of expenditures. References; appendixes on classification of institutional funds and on educational and general expenditures.

MOON, R. G. "Beating the High Cost of Low Ratios." *Liberal*

Education, 1971, *57,* 160–166. Increased faculty productivity is of highest priority to achieve optimal uses of resources in the next decade.

MORISHIMA, J. K. (Ed.) *An Annotated Bibliography of Institutional Research 1970–71.* Berkeley: Office of Institutional Research, University of California, 1971. Contains 183 citations, including the following categories: goals and long-range planning; curriculum and instruction; space utilization and scheduling; characteristics of entering students; general student characteristics; recruitment and admissions; prediction and academic performance; perception of college environment; retention, attrition, and transfer. See also bibliographies annotated and compiled by Cameron Fincher (1968–69) and Morishima (1969–70), also published by the Office of Educational Research.

O'NEILL, J. *Resource Use in Higher Education: Trends in Output and Inputs, 1930 to 1967.* Berkeley: Carnegie Commission on Higher Education, 1971. Develops useful technical knowledge about long-run trends in real resource costs per unit of output in American higher education, concentrating mainly on units of student instruction (credit hours). Examines ways of measuring current operating expenditures. Needed are better ways of measuring the quality of credit hours and the quality of output.

ROURKE, F. E., AND BROOKS, G. E. *The Managerial Revolution in Higher Education.* Baltimore: Johns Hopkins Press, 1966. An integral part of the managerial revolution of the last ten years, institutional research is a variegated form of organizational self-study designed to help colleges and universities gather an expanding range of information about their own internal operations and the effectiveness with which they are using their own resources. Certain strengths and weaknesses of institutional research are covered.

SCHIETINGER, E. F. (Ed.) *Introductory Papers on Institutional Research.* Atlanta, Ga.: Southern Regional Education Board, 1968. A comprehensive series of articles on the continuing role of institutional research in academic analysis, programming, and planning—focusing on the institution rather than upon higher education in general. Contributors are W. Hugh Stickler, John E. Stecklein, Cameron Fincher, James L. Miller, and L. Joseph Lins, participants in an SREB workshop on the pragmatic operation of institutional research on any campus. Bibliographies are appended to each article.

STECKLEIN, J. E. "Institutional Research." In Asa S. Knowles (Ed.), *Handbook of College and University Administration.* Vol. I. New York: McGraw-Hill, 1970. Pp. 4–23. A general overview of the history, functions and scope, organization and administration, and neglected areas of institutional research. Brief bibliography.

WITMER, D. R. "Cost Studies in Higher Education." *Review of Educational Research,* 1972, *42,* 99–127. A summary of the literature on cost analysis. Subtopics include (a) financial accounting in higher education; (b) registrars' records: the units in unit cost studies; (c) cost studies, historically; (d) current cost concepts; and (e) recent cost studies and procedural guides. Extensive bibliography appended.

Index

A

Accreditation: of studied colleges, 8; and use of cost analysis data, 101, 102-103, 112
Administrators, 168, 169-170
Admissions. *See* Recruitment and admissions
Alumni: cost analysis data used by, 102, 111; in effectiveness analysis, 83, 86, 90-91, 92-93, 95, 96

ASTIN, A. W., 8, 74, 169, 176
Attrition, reduction of, 169

B

BINNING, D. W., 169, 177
BLISCHKE, W., 3, 187
BOBBITT, F., 76-77
BOGARD, L., 79, 177
BOWEN, H. R., 74, 75, 78, 79, 159, 169, 171, 177, 198-199
BRICK, M., 158

203

C

CALLAHAN, R., 76, 77, 179
Carnegie Commission on Higher Education, 8, 43, 70, 179
Catalogs, use of in recruitment, 68-69
Change: resistance to, 1-5; strategies for, 164-165
Class size: cost analysis impact on, 104, 105; cost analysis of, 30-33; cost relationships of, 42; guidelines for, 172; in planning strategy, 128-130
Colleges: assumptions about, 163-164; in effectiveness analysis, 83-85, 90, 92, 94-95; goals of, 144-145, 155-157; problems of, 155-162; in study, 8-9
Consortia: and cost analysis data, 102, 116; for effectiveness, 164, 168
Cost: formula for, 43-46; per student credit hour, 33, 35-41; relationships of, 41-43
Cost accounting, 123-124
Cost analysis: bibliography on, 198-202; changes resulting from, 104-107; of curricula, ix-x, 6-46; data development for, 103-104; data use in, case studies of, 112-119; data use in, strategies for, 107-112; groups using, 100-103; history of, 2; strategy for in long-range planning, 123-128; uses of, 99-119
Cost-benefit, 124-125
Cost-effectiveness, 124-128
Council for the Advancement of Small Colleges, ix-x, xii, xiii, 8, 117, 123
Courses taught: cost analysis impact on, 104, 106, 107-109; cost analysis of, 20, 22-26, 27; data collection form for, 148-150; limit to, 171-172
Credit-hour distribution, 13-18
Current operations, 33-46
Curricula, cost analysis of, ix-x, 6-46

D

Deficits, unfunded scholarships related to, 56-58
Development office, cost analysis of, 60-64
Distinctiveness as purpose, 155-156
DOUGLASS, G. K., 74, 75, 78, 169, 171, 177, 199
DRESSEL, P. L., 144, 158, 180, 194
DRUCKER, P., 80, 181

E

Effectiveness: case studies of, 89-98; concept of, 79-82; efficiency related to, 74-98; as purpose, 162-166; recommendations for, 154-173
Efficiency: concept of, 76-79; effectiveness related to, 74-98
EMERSON, H., 77, 181
Enrollment: cost analysis data impact on, 104; cost analysis of, 12-13; cost relationships of, 43; data collection form for, 149, 151; increase of, 155, 169
Excellence as purpose, 156-157
Expenditures: data collection form for, 148-149, 151-153; for development office, 62-63; distribution of, 47-58; educational and general, 53-56, 141; income related to, 170-171; percentages of, 50-51

F

Faculty: compensation of, 29-30, 43, 141, 148, 149; cost analysis data used by, 105, 111, 113-114; cost analysis impact on, 104, 106; cost analysis of, 26, 28-30; in effectiveness analysis, 83-85, 89, 92, 94, 97; flexibility of, 167; full-time, ratio of to part-time, 166-167; full-time equivalent, 130-131; productivity of, 28-29, 42, 109-110, 137; size of, 168

Faculty-student ratio: enrollment related to, 13; in planning strategy, 137; recommended, 172

G

Grants, cost analysis data used in proposals for, 101, 102, 111-112

H

HARRIS, S., 44, 101, 182
HAUSRATH, R., xiii
HOBBS, W., xiii
HODGKINSON, H., xiii
Humanities. *See* Subject areas
HUNGATE, T. L., x, 8, 15, 25, 30, 33, 43, 46, 55, 183

I

IDZERDA, S., xiii
IKENBERRY, S. O., 80, 183
Income: data collection form for, 149, 152-153; educational and general, 51-53; expenditures related to, 170-171; percentages of, 49-50; sources of, 47-58
Institutional Functioning Inventory, 86-88, 91, 93, 96
Institutional research: bibliography on, 198-202; cost analysis data use in, 117-119; for effectiveness, 167-168; in long-range planning, 122-123
Institutional size. *See* Enrollment

J

JELLEMA, W., xiii, 74, 157, 183, 200
JOHNSON, D. L., 70, 73, 184

K

KNOTT, R. E., xiii, 74-98

L

LE LONG, D., 78, 185
LEE, C. B. T., 8, 74, 176
LEHMAN, T., 3, 187
LeTourneau Foundation, x, xiii

Liberal arts education, changing demand for, 158-159
LITTERER, J., 77-78, 185

M

MC GRATH, E. J., ix, 74, 75, 158
Majors: cost analysis impact on, 104, 105, 109-110; cost analysis of, 18-21; cost relationships of, 42; data collection form for, 148, 150; number of, 172
Management, effectiveness related to, 160-166
Methodoloy: for cost analysis, 9-12; for effectiveness analysis, 82-89; problems of, 11-12
MOON, R. G., 79, 186, 200-201

N

Natural sciences. *See* Subject areas

P

PACE, C. R., 8, 187
PALOLA, E., 3, 187
PIPITONE, R., xiii
Planning, long-range: advantages and disadvantages of, 146-147; bibliography for, 193-198; cost analysis data for, 100, 106, 115-119; cost analysis strategy for, 123-128; data analysis and interpretation for, 122-123; data base for, 120-121, 148-153; data collection forms for, 147-153; for effectiveness, 168; resistance to, 1-5; strategy for, 120-153
Professional subjects. *See* Subject areas
Program budgeting: cost analysis data for, 110-111; for long-range planning, 125
Publications for recruitment, 68-69
Purchasing for effectiveness, 171

R

RANCE, J., xiv
Records, keeping of, 121

Recruitment and admissions: contacts and applicants in, 65-68;
cost analysis of, 64-73; income and expense of, 71-72;
publications for, 68-69; staff
for, 69-71
Risk capital in development office,
63-64

S

Scholarships, unfunded, related to
deficits, 56-58
SHOEMAKER, W., 123
Sloan Foundation, Alfred P., x, xiii
SMITH, H. K., 3
SMITH, V. B., 170, 189
Social sciences. *See* Subject areas
SPAULDING, F., 76
SPENCE, D., xiii
Sterling College, 107-108, 109-110
Student credit hour: cost per, 33, 35-
41; distribution of, 16-18; fac-
ulty time per, 141-142; in
planning strategy, 137
Students: cost analysis data used by,
102, 111, 113-114; cost per,
40-41, 105, 141; cost relation-
ships per, 42; in effectiveness
analysis, 83-85, 90, 92, 93-95

STUIT, D., 81, 190
Subject areas: credit-hour distribution in, 13-15, 17; cost per
student credit hour in, 35-38;
courses omitted from, 10-11;
courses taught in, 22-24, 27;
majors in, 18-20; teaching load
in, 28; planning strategy for,
132-138

T

TAYLOR, F., 76
Teaching load: cost analysis of, 26,
28-29; in planning strategy,
130-136
TICKTON, S. G., ix
TOFFLER, A., 3, 190
Trustees, cost analysis data used by,
100-101, 111, 113-114, 115-116

V

VOSKUYL, R. J., ix-x, xiii

W

WEBBER, R., xiii
WERKEMA, G., xiii
WITMER, D. R., 2, 192, 202